A JOURNEY THROUGH THE A TO Z OF DEEP LEARNING: UNLOCKING THE DEPTHS OF INTELLIGENCE

S. Begum

S. Begum

A Journey Through the A to Z of Deep Learning: Unlocking the Depths of Intelligence

S. Begum

CONTENTS

A to Z of Deep Learning

S. Begum

INTRODUCTION

WELCOME TO THE WORLD OF DEEP LEARNING

In the vast landscape of technology and artificial intelligence, there exists a domain that has revolutionized our understanding of intelligence itself: Deep Learning. This book, "A Journey Through the A to Z of Deep Learning: Unlocking the Depths of Intelligence," is your key to unlocking the mysteries and potential of this remarkable field.

THE POWER OF UNLOCKING INTELLIGENCE

Deep Learning, a subset of machine learning, has emerged as a transformative force in the realm of artificial intelligence. It has enabled computers to perform tasks that were once deemed the exclusive domain of human intellect, such as image recognition, natural language understanding, and even playing complex games like chess and Go. But what makes deep learning truly remarkable is its ability to extract meaningful patterns and representations from vast amounts of data, enabling it to learn and adapt in ways that were previously inconceivable.

Imagine a world where machines can understand and interpret the nuances of human language, diagnose diseases with unprecedented accuracy, drive vehicles autonomously, and assist in scientific discoveries that were once beyond our reach. This is the world that deep learning is shaping, and it's a world that you can be a part of.

A to Z of Deep Learning

NAVIGATING THE A TO Z OF DEEP LEARNING

In this journey, we will explore the A to Z of deep learning, breaking down complex concepts into digestible pieces that anyone, from curious beginners to seasoned professionals, can grasp. We'll start with the fundamentals, unraveling the core principles and mathematics that underpin deep learning. From there, we'll delve into practical aspects, including setting up your deep learning environment and working with data.

Each chapter of this book is designed to build your understanding progressively. We'll cover topics like activation functions, backpropagation, convolutional neural networks (CNNs), deep learning frameworks, and the ethical considerations surrounding this powerful technology. Along the way, you'll find hands-on projects and real-world applications that will allow you to put your newfound knowledge into practice.

Our journey will culminate in a glimpse of the future, exploring emerging trends and technologies that are set to shape the next generation of deep learning. We'll also provide you with a glossary of deep learning terms to demystify the jargon that often surrounds this field.

Whether you're an aspiring data scientist, a curious hobbyist, or simply someone intrigued by the wonders of artificial intelligence, this book is your passport to the exciting world of deep learning. So, fasten your seatbelt, and let's embark on this exhilarating journey together as we unlock the depths of intelligence through the A to Z of deep learning.

CHAPTER 1: THE FOUNDATION OF DEEP LEARNING

1.1. WHAT IS DEEP LEARNING?

In the grand tapestry of artificial intelligence, deep learning emerges as a dazzling thread—a potent technique that has revolutionized our understanding of how machines can learn and think. At its core, deep learning is an intricate subset of machine learning, but its prowess lies in its ability to mimic the human brain's neural architecture, thereby enabling computers to fathom complex patterns, make decisions, and generate insights with an uncanny finesse.

At its essence, deep learning models are constructed from artificial neural networks. These networks, inspired by the intricate web of neurons in our brains, consist of layers upon layers of interconnected nodes, each harboring its own set of parameters. It's within this labyrinthine structure that deep learning models glean meaning from data.

What sets deep learning apart from conventional machine learning is its capacity to autonomously learn from data hierarchically. In other words, deep learning systems can sift through raw data, identify low-level features, and progressively build a nuanced understanding of higher-level abstractions. This capability lends itself to a multitude of applications, from image recognition and natural language processing to autonomous driving and healthcare diagnostics.

A to Z of Deep Learning

The fundamental driving force behind deep learning's meteoric rise is the advent of ample computing power and copious datasets. With the brawn of modern GPUs and access to mountains of data, deep learning models can be trained to achieve astonishing feats, defying the boundaries of what was once deemed impossible.

As we traverse the chapters of this book, we shall embark on a captivating journey through the very fabric of deep learning. We will demystify its inner workings, explore its practical applications, and contemplate the profound ethical considerations that accompany its ascendancy. With each step, we'll uncover the intricate tapestry of intelligence that deep learning weaves, offering you a glimpse into the limitless possibilities that lie ahead in our quest to unlock the depths of intelligence.

1.2. NEURAL NETWORKS: THE BUILDING BLOCKS

In our exploration of the A to Z of deep learning, it is imperative to begin with the foundational elements that underpin this transformative field. At the very heart of deep learning lies the concept of neural networks, often referred to as the building blocks of artificial intelligence.

Imagine the human brain, with its intricate network of neurons and synapses—a marvel of nature's design. Neural networks in deep learning aim to mimic this biological structure, albeit in a simplified and highly abstracted form. They are the computational model that empowers machines to learn from data, make predictions, and even perform tasks that were once considered the exclusive domain of human intelligence.

At its essence, a neural network comprises layers of interconnected nodes, known as neurons. These neurons are organized into input, hidden, and output layers, each serving a distinct purpose in the learning process. The magic happens when these neurons communicate with each other through weighted connections, where the strength of each connection determines its significance in the network's decision-making.

The journey through neural networks is a fascinating one, and it's crucial to understand their role as the bedrock of deep learning. As we delve deeper into this topic, we will explore various types of neural networks, from the fundamental feedforward networks to the more intricate recurrent and convolutional architectures. Each type serves a unique purpose, making them indispensable tools in solving a wide range of real-world problems.

In the chapters that follow, we will embark on a journey through the intricacies of neural networks, unveiling their inner workings and demystifying the complexities that make them such potent instruments in the world of artificial intelligence. By the end of this exploration, you'll have a profound understanding of how these building blocks come together to unlock the depths of intelligence in the realm of deep learning.

1.3. HISTORICAL MILESTONES IN DEEP LEARNING

The evolution of deep learning has been punctuated by several groundbreaking milestones that have propelled the field into the forefront of artificial intelligence. These historical moments serve as signposts in the journey of unlocking the depths of intelligence. Let us delve into some of the most pivotal milestones in the history of deep learning.

1943 - McCulloch-Pitts Neuron:
The foundation of artificial neural networks was laid with the McCulloch-Pitts neuron model. Proposed by Warren McCulloch and Walter Pitts, this conceptual model mimicked the workings of a biological neuron, creating the basis for future neural network development.

1956 - Dartmouth Workshop:
Often regarded as the birth of artificial intelligence, the Dartmouth Workshop convened by John McCarthy and Marvin Minsky brought together pioneers who aimed to develop machines that could simulate human intelligence. Although not solely focused on deep learning, this event marked the beginning of the quest for intelligent machines.

1986 - Backpropagation Algorithm:
The development of the backpropagation algorithm by Geoffrey Hinton, David Rumelhart, and Ronald Williams revolutionized the training of neural networks. This mathematical technique allowed networks to adjust their internal parameters, making them capable of learning and adapting from data.

2012 - ImageNet and AlexNet:
The ImageNet Large Scale Visual Recognition Challenge and the AlexNet architecture, designed by Alex Krizhevsky, marked a watershed moment in computer vision. AlexNet's victory at the ImageNet challenge demonstrated the power of deep convolutional neural networks in image classification tasks, sparking renewed interest in deep learning.

2015 - DeepMind's AlphaGo:
AlphaGo, developed by DeepMind, showcased the potential of deep reinforcement learning by defeating world champion Go player Lee Sedol. This milestone highlighted the applicability of deep learning beyond traditional domains, extending its reach to complex strategy games.

2019 - GPT-2 and Transformer Models:
The release of OpenAI's GPT-2, a transformer-based language model, signaled a breakthrough in natural language processing. GPT-2 demonstrated the generation of coherent and contextually relevant text, setting the stage for subsequent advancements in AI-driven language understanding.

2020 - Deep Learning in Healthcare:
The COVID-19 pandemic accelerated the adoption of deep learning in healthcare. AI models were deployed for tasks such as diagnosing COVID-19 from medical images and predicting patient outcomes, showcasing the potential of deep learning to transform healthcare systems worldwide.

These historical milestones represent only a fraction of the rich tapestry that is deep learning's history. Each achievement has contributed to the advancement of the field, pushing the boundaries of what machines can achieve and offering a glimpse into a future where artificial intelligence plays an increasingly vital role in our lives. In the following chapters, we will explore these milestones and the underlying principles that drive deep learning's progress.

1.4. WHY DEEP LEARNING MATTERS

In our rapidly evolving technological landscape, the significance of deep learning cannot be overstated. But what precisely makes deep learning so vital? This section will delve into the profound impact and relevance of deep learning in our world today.

Deep learning matters because it represents a revolutionary paradigm shift in artificial intelligence. Unlike traditional rule-based systems, deep learning models can learn directly from data, extracting intricate patterns and representations that were previously beyond the reach of conventional algorithms.

At the core of deep learning's importance is its ability to process vast amounts of data with unprecedented speed and accuracy. Whether it's recognizing faces in photos, translating languages in real-time, or diagnosing medical conditions from images, deep learning systems excel at tasks that demand a nuanced understanding of complex information.

Moreover, deep learning has democratized AI research and application. Open-source frameworks like TensorFlow and PyTorch have empowered developers and researchers worldwide to harness the potential of deep learning, making it accessible to a broader audience. This democratization has led to innovations in various domains, from autonomous vehicles to healthcare.

Deep learning is also driving advancements in natural language processing, enabling machines to understand and generate human language. This capability has revolutionized chatbots, language translation, and content generation, transforming the way we interact with computers.

Another compelling reason why deep learning matters is its role in personalization. Recommendation systems powered by deep learning algorithms curate content and products tailored to individual preferences, enhancing user experiences across the internet.

Furthermore, the applications of deep learning continue to expand. From assisting scientists in drug discovery to optimizing supply chains in business, its versatility knows no bounds. Deep learning is a driving force behind the Fourth Industrial Revolution, reshaping industries and economies.

In essence, deep learning matters because it empowers machines with the ability to learn, adapt, and make decisions akin to human intelligence. Its far-reaching implications touch every aspect of our lives, from how we shop online to how we receive medical diagnoses. As we journey through the A to Z of deep learning, you will discover the profound ways in which this technology is shaping our present and future.

CHAPTER 2: GETTING STARTED WITH DEEP LEARNING

2.1. SETTING UP YOUR DEEP LEARNING ENVIRONMENT

In the exciting world of deep learning, one of the first steps on your journey involves setting up your environment. This environment will serve as your workshop, your laboratory, where you'll create, experiment, and fine-tune your neural networks. In this section, we'll guide you through the essential steps of creating a robust deep learning environment.

2.1.1. CHOOSING YOUR DEVELOPMENT PLATFORM

Before diving into the technical details, you'll need to choose the development platform that best suits your needs. There are several options available, but two of the most popular choices are TensorFlow and PyTorch. Let's briefly discuss each:

TensorFlow: Developed by Google, TensorFlow is known for its scalability and flexibility. It's an excellent choice for both beginners and experts, with a vast community and a wealth of resources.

PyTorch: PyTorch, developed by Facebook's AI Research lab (FAIR), has gained immense popularity among researchers due to its dynamic computation graph and ease of use. It's particularly well-suited for experimentation and research.

The choice between TensorFlow and PyTorch often comes down to personal preference and specific project requirements. Whichever you choose, the following steps will guide you through setting up your environment.

2.1.2. INSTALLING PYTHON

Python is the lingua franca of the deep learning world. Most deep learning frameworks, including TensorFlow and PyTorch, are built to work seamlessly with Python. If you don't have Python installed, download and install it from the official Python website (https://www.python.org/downloads/).

Ensure that you're using Python 3.x, as Python 2.x is no longer supported.

2.1.3. INSTALLING DEEP LEARNING FRAMEWORKS

Once Python is installed, the next step is to install your chosen deep learning framework. We'll provide instructions for both TensorFlow and PyTorch.

Installing TensorFlow

To install TensorFlow, open your terminal or command prompt and run the following command:

pip install tensorflow

A to Z of Deep Learning

This command will download and install the latest version of TensorFlow.

Installing PyTorch

For PyTorch, you can use pip as well. Run the following command:

pip install torch

This command will install the CPU-only version of PyTorch. If you have a compatible GPU and want to leverage its power, you can install the GPU version by following the instructions on the PyTorch website (https://pytorch.org/get-started/locally/).

2.1.4. VERIFYING YOUR INSTALLATION

After the installation is complete, it's a good practice to verify that everything is set up correctly. You can do this by opening a Python interpreter and importing the deep learning framework you installed.

For TensorFlow:

import tensorflow as tf

print("TensorFlow version:", tf.__version__)

For PyTorch:

S. Begum

```
import torch

print("PyTorch version:", torch.__version__)
```

If you see the version numbers printed without any errors, congratulations! Your deep learning environment is ready for action.

In the next section, we'll explore the essential Python libraries that complement your deep learning environment and prepare you for your journey into the world of neural networks.

2.2. ESSENTIAL PYTHON LIBRARIES FOR DEEP LEARNING**

In our journey through the A to Z of deep learning, we now come to a critical juncture: selecting the essential Python libraries that will empower us to delve into the fascinating world of neural networks and machine learning. Python has emerged as the lingua franca of the AI community, thanks to its versatility and a wealth of libraries specifically designed for deep learning. In this chapter, we will introduce you to some of the most indispensable Python libraries that will be your companions throughout this journey.

2.2.1. NUMPY: THE FOUNDATION OF SCIENTIFIC COMPUTING

Before we dive into the world of deep learning, we need a strong foundation in scientific computing. NumPy, short for Numerical Python, is the bedrock of scientific

A to Z of Deep Learning

computing in Python. It provides support for large, multi-dimensional arrays and matrices, along with a vast collection of high-level mathematical functions to operate on these arrays. NumPy is essential because most deep learning libraries, such as TensorFlow and PyTorch, rely on it as their base.

Let's take a look at a simple example of how NumPy can be used to perform basic operations:

```python
import numpy as np


# Creating NumPy arrays

a = np.array([1, 2, 3])

b = np.array([4, 5, 6])


# Element-wise addition

result = a + b

print("Result of addition:", result)
```

2.2.2. TENSORFLOW: GOOGLE'S DEEP LEARNING FRAMEWORK

TensorFlow is a powerful open-source deep learning library developed by Google Brain. It's renowned for its flexibility and scalability, making it an excellent choice for both beginners and experts. TensorFlow allows you to build and train various machine learning models, including neural networks, with ease.

Here's a snippet demonstrating how to create a simple neural network using TensorFlow:

```
import tensorflow as tf


# Define a sequential model

model = tf.keras.Sequential([

    tf.keras.layers.Dense(64, activation='relu',
input_shape=(784,)),

    tf.keras.layers.Dense(10,
activation='softmax')

])

# Compile the model

model.compile(optimizer='adam',

        loss='sparse_categorical_crossentropy',

        metrics=['accuracy'])

# Print model summary

model.summary()
```

2.2.3. PYTORCH: THE RESEARCHER'S CHOICE

PyTorch is another prominent deep learning library, highly favored by researchers due to its dynamic computational graph and ease of debugging. Developed by Facebook's AI Research lab (FAIR), PyTorch empowers you to build dynamic neural networks, making it an excellent choice for cutting-edge research.

Let's create a simple neural network using PyTorch:

```python
import torch

import torch.nn as nn

# Define a custom neural network class

class SimpleNN(nn.Module):

    def __init__(self):

        super(SimpleNN, self).__init__()

        self.fc1 = nn.Linear(784, 64)

        self.fc2 = nn.Linear(64, 10)

    def forward(self, x):

        x = torch.relu(self.fc1(x))

        x = torch.softmax(self.fc2(x), dim=1)

        return x
```

```
# Create an instance of the neural network

model = SimpleNN()

# Print the model architecture

print(model)
```

These libraries, NumPy, TensorFlow, and PyTorch, form the cornerstone of deep learning in Python. Familiarizing yourself with them will set the stage for our journey through the depths of intelligence, enabling you to build and train intricate neural networks as we progress through this book. In the following chapters, we will delve deeper into each of these libraries and explore their capabilities in greater detail.

2.3. DATA: THE LIFEBLOOD OF DEEP LEARNING

In the realm of deep learning, data is the lifeblood that fuels the intelligence of neural networks. Without quality data, even the most sophisticated algorithms and architectures would falter. In this section, we'll delve into the crucial role data plays in deep learning and explore how to prepare, preprocess, and augment data to make it suitable for training deep neural networks.

UNDERSTANDING THE SIGNIFICANCE OF DATA

Deep learning models are designed to learn from data, and the quality and quantity of data you provide can make or break your model's performance. The more diverse, representative, and abundant your dataset is, the better your model will generalize to unseen examples.

Consider an image recognition task where you want a neural network to identify various species of flowers. To accomplish this, you need a dataset containing a wide variety of flower images, each labeled with the corresponding species. The neural network learns to recognize patterns and features from these images during the training process.

DATA PREPROCESSING

Before feeding data into a deep learning model, it's essential to preprocess it to ensure it's in a suitable format. Data preprocessing typically involves the following steps:

1. Data Cleaning: Identifying and handling missing values, outliers, and anomalies in the dataset.

2. Data Normalization: Scaling features to have similar ranges, often between 0 and 1, to help the model converge faster.

3. Data Augmentation: Creating new training examples by applying transformations like rotation, cropping, or adding noise. This increases the model's robustness.

Let's take a look at a code snippet in Python using the popular library TensorFlow to perform data normalization:

```
import tensorflow as tf
```

S. Begum

```python
from tensorflow.keras.preprocessing.image
import ImageDataGenerator


# Load your dataset

(train_images, train_labels), (test_images,
test_labels) =
tf.keras.datasets.cifar10.load_data()


# Normalize pixel values to be between 0 and 1

train_images, test_images = train_images /
255.0, test_images / 255.0
```

DATA AUGMENTATION

Data augmentation is a powerful technique, especially in computer vision tasks, to artificially expand your dataset. It helps prevent overfitting by exposing the model to a wider range of variations in the training data. Here's an example of data augmentation in TensorFlow:

```python
# Create an ImageDataGenerator for data
augmentation

datagen = ImageDataGenerator(

  rotation_range=40,

  width_shift_range=0.2,
```

```
        height_shift_range=0.2,

        shear_range=0.2,

        zoom_range=0.2,

        horizontal_flip=True,

        fill_mode='nearest'

    )

    # Apply data augmentation to a single image

    augmented_image =
    datagen.random_transform(train_images[0])
```

In this code, we're applying random rotations, shifts, shearing, zooming, and horizontal flips to an image.

Data is undeniably the cornerstone of deep learning. By understanding its importance and mastering the art of data preprocessing and augmentation, you pave the way for training robust and accurate deep learning models. In the subsequent chapters, we'll delve deeper into the technical aspects of building and training neural networks.

CHAPTER 3: A FOR ACTIVATION FUNCTIONS

3.1. UNDERSTANDING ACTIVATION FUNCTIONS

In the realm of deep learning, activation functions are the pivotal cogs in the neural network machinery. These functions introduce non-linearity to the network, enabling it to learn complex patterns and make sense of intricate data. In this section, we'll delve into the core concepts behind activation functions and explore their significance in the training process.

THE ROLE OF ACTIVATION FUNCTIONS

At its essence, a neural network is a composition of interconnected neurons, each mimicking the behavior of biological neurons in the human brain. These artificial neurons take in inputs, perform mathematical operations, and produce outputs. Activation functions come into play during the 'perceptron' stage of each neuron, where they determine whether the neuron should 'fire' (activate) or remain dormant.

Activation functions serve several critical purposes:

1. Introducing Non-linearity: Without activation functions, a neural network would be no more powerful than a linear regression model. Activation functions add complexity, enabling the network to model non-linear relationships within data, a capability crucial for tasks like image recognition and natural language processing.

2. Normalization: Activation functions normalize the output of a neuron, often restricting it to a specific range. This normalization helps in stabilizing and speeding up the training process, preventing the network from converging too quickly or too slowly.

3. Learning Complex Patterns: By introducing non-linearity, activation functions allow neural networks to learn and represent intricate patterns in data, such as the edges, textures, and shapes in an image.

COMMON ACTIVATION FUNCTIONS

There are various activation functions used in deep learning, each with its own characteristics. Here are some of the most common ones:

- Sigmoid Function: The sigmoid function squashes its input into a range between 0 and 1. It was historically popular but has been largely replaced by others due to some limitations like vanishing gradients.

- Hyperbolic Tangent (Tanh) Function: Similar to the sigmoid function, the tanh function maps inputs to a range between -1 and 1. It addresses some of the vanishing gradient issues but not all.

- Rectified Linear Unit (ReLU): ReLU has gained immense popularity. It returns zero for negative inputs and passes positive inputs as they are. This function effectively mitigates vanishing gradients and accelerates training.

- Leaky ReLU: To address the 'dying ReLU' problem where some neurons never activate, the leaky ReLU allows a small,

S. Begum

non-zero gradient for negative inputs, ensuring all neurons learn.

- Exponential Linear Unit (ELU): ELU is another variant of ReLU that mitigates the 'dying ReLU' problem while providing smoother gradients than Leaky ReLU.

CODE SNIPPET - IMPLEMENTING ACTIVATION FUNCTIONS IN PYTHON

Here's a Python code snippet illustrating how to implement some common activation functions:

```python
import numpy as np


def sigmoid(x):
    return 1 / (1 + np.exp(-x))


def tanh(x):
    return np.tanh(x)


def relu(x):
    return np.maximum(0, x)

def leaky_relu(x, alpha=0.01):
```

```
        return np.where(x > 0, x, alpha * x)



    def elu(x, alpha=1.0):

        return np.where(x > 0, x, alpha * (np.exp(x)
    - 1))
```

These functions are the building blocks of deep learning, and understanding their properties is essential as we progress through the A to Z of deep learning. In the following sections, we'll explore each of these activation functions in greater detail and discuss when and where to use them in your neural network architectures.

Now that we have introduced the fundamental concepts behind activation functions and their significance, let's delve deeper into some of the common activation functions used in deep learning and understand their characteristics and use cases.

SIGMOID FUNCTION

The sigmoid function, denoted as σ(x), is one of the earliest activation functions used in neural networks. It has a characteristic S-shaped curve that maps input values to a range between 0 and 1. Mathematically, the sigmoid function is defined as:

$$\sigma(x) = \frac{1}{1 + e^{-x}}$$

The sigmoid function is suitable for binary classification problems where the output needs to represent probabilities. However, it has limitations, such as vanishing gradients during training, which can slow down convergence in deep networks.

HYPERBOLIC TANGENT (TANH) FUNCTION

The hyperbolic tangent function, tanh(x), is similar to the sigmoid but maps inputs to a range between -1 and 1. It is defined as:

$$\tanh(x) = \frac{e^x - e^{-x}}{e^x + e^{-x}}$$

Tanh addresses some of the vanishing gradient issues of the sigmoid function and is often used in hidden layers of neural networks. However, it still suffers from vanishing gradients for extremely large or small input values.

RECTIFIED LINEAR UNIT (RELU)

ReLU, represented as f(x) = max(0, x), has gained prominence in recent years due to its effectiveness in mitigating vanishing gradient problems. It replaces all negative values with zero and leaves positive values unchanged. Mathematically, it can be defined as:

$$f(x) = \begin{cases} x, & \text{if } x > 0 \\ 0, & \text{otherwise} \end{cases}$$

ReLU is computationally efficient and helps accelerate training, making it a popular choice for activation in many neural network architectures.

LEAKY RELU

Leaky ReLU is an improvement over the standard ReLU. It allows a small, non-zero gradient for negative inputs, preventing some neurons from becoming inactive during training. The function is defined as:

$$f(x) = \begin{cases} x, & \text{if } x > 0 \\ \alpha x, & \text{otherwise} \end{cases}$$

Here, α is a small positive constant. Leaky ReLU is particularly useful when you want to avoid the "dying ReLU" problem, where neurons stop learning.

EXPONENTIAL LINEAR UNIT (ELU)

ELU is another variant of ReLU that addresses the dying ReLU problem while providing smoother gradients. It is defined as:

$$f(x) = \begin{cases} x, & \text{if } x > 0 \\ \alpha \cdot (e^x - 1), & \text{otherwise} \end{cases}$$

The parameter α determines the slope of the function for negative inputs. ELU has become increasingly popular due to its ability to handle the drawbacks of both ReLU and Leaky ReLU.

In the upcoming sections of this chapter, we will explore these activation functions in greater detail, including their mathematical properties, advantages, and scenarios in which they excel. Understanding these activation functions is essential for effectively designing and training deep neural networks.

3.2. SIGMOID AND HYPERBOLIC TANGENT FUNCTIONS

In our quest to understand the foundational components of deep learning, we now turn our attention to activation functions, which play a pivotal role in shaping the behavior of neural networks. Activation functions are non-linear transformations that introduce non-linearity into the model, allowing it to learn complex relationships between input and output data. In this section, we will delve into two classic activation functions: the Sigmoid and Hyperbolic Tangent functions.

3.2.1. THE SIGMOID FUNCTION

The Sigmoid function, also known as the logistic function, is one of the earliest activation functions used in artificial

A to Z of Deep Learning

neural networks. It maps any real-valued number to a value between 0 and 1. The formula for the Sigmoid function is as follows:

$$\sigma(x) = 1 / (1 + e^{\wedge}(-x))$$

Here, `σ(x)` represents the output of the Sigmoid function when given the input `x`, and `e` is the base of the natural logarithm (approximately equal to 2.71828). The Sigmoid function has an S-shaped curve, which makes it suitable for problems where we want to model the probability of an event occurring. For instance, in binary classification problems, the Sigmoid function can be used to predict the probability of an input belonging to one of the two classes.

Let's visualize the Sigmoid function using Python:

```
import numpy as np

import matplotlib.pyplot as plt

def sigmoid(x):

    return 1 / (1 + np.exp(-x))

x = np.linspace(-6, 6, 100)

y = sigmoid(x)

plt.figure(figsize=(8, 6))

plt.plot(x, y, label='Sigmoid Function',
color='blue')
```

```
plt.xlabel('Input')

plt.ylabel('Output')

plt.title('Sigmoid Function')

plt.grid(True)

plt.legend()

plt.show()
```

In the code snippet above, we define the Sigmoid function and then plot it over a range of input values. The resulting graph illustrates the S-shaped curve characteristic of the Sigmoid function.

3.2.2. THE HYPERBOLIC TANGENT FUNCTION

The Hyperbolic Tangent function, often referred to as Tanh, is another activation function that maps input values to a range between -1 and 1. It is defined by the following formula:

$$tanh(x) = (e^{\wedge}(x) - e^{\wedge}(-x)) / (e^{\wedge}(x) + e^{\wedge}(-x))$$

Similar to the Sigmoid function, Tanh is also S-shaped but centered around the origin. It is particularly useful in situations where the data has negative values, as it can capture both positive and negative correlations effectively.

A to Z of Deep Learning
To visualize the Tanh function using Python:

```python
import numpy as np
import matplotlib.pyplot as plt

def tanh(x):

    return np.tanh(x)

x = np.linspace(-6, 6, 100)

y = tanh(x)

plt.figure(figsize=(8, 6))

plt.plot(x, y, label='Tanh Function',
color='red')

plt.xlabel('Input')

plt.ylabel('Output')

plt.title('Tanh Function')

plt.grid(True)

plt.legend()

plt.show()
```

In this code, we define the Tanh function and plot it, showcasing its characteristics.

Both the Sigmoid and Tanh functions have been historically important in deep learning, but they are not without their limitations. For instance, they suffer from the vanishing gradient problem, which can impede the training of very deep neural networks. Nevertheless, understanding these fundamental activation functions is crucial as they form the basis for more advanced activations used in modern deep learning architectures.

3.2.3. PRACTICAL CONSIDERATIONS

While the Sigmoid and Tanh functions were once popular choices for activation functions, they are now less commonly used in deep neural networks. This is due to some of their limitations, such as the vanishing gradient problem, which can hinder the training of deep networks. In practice, modern architectures often favor activation functions like the Rectified Linear Unit (ReLU) and its variants, which tend to mitigate these issues.

However, understanding the Sigmoid and Tanh functions remains valuable for several reasons:

- Historical Significance: These functions played a pivotal role in the early development of neural networks and serve as important milestones in the field's history.

- Specific Use Cases: There are scenarios, such as binary classification tasks and certain recurrent neural networks (RNNs), where the Sigmoid and Tanh functions can still find relevance.

- Building Blocks: The concepts and mathematical properties of these functions serve as a foundation for understanding more complex activation functions.

A to Z of Deep Learning

As you delve deeper into the world of deep learning, you'll encounter a diverse range of activation functions, each tailored to specific challenges and objectives. It's essential to choose the right activation function based on the characteristics of your data and the nature of your problem.

In the upcoming chapters, we will explore advanced activation functions and dive into practical examples of when and how to use them effectively. Additionally, we'll discuss techniques to address the vanishing gradient problem and other challenges associated with training deep neural networks.

In this section, we have introduced two fundamental activation functions in deep learning: the Sigmoid and Hyperbolic Tangent functions. While these functions have been overshadowed by newer activations like ReLU, they remain valuable tools in understanding the historical and foundational aspects of neural networks.

As you progress through this journey, keep in mind that the choice of activation function is just one piece of the deep learning puzzle. Our exploration will continue as we delve into more complex concepts and practical applications of deep learning, equipping you with the knowledge and skills to unlock the full potential of artificial intelligence.

3.3. THE POWER OF RECTIFIED LINEAR UNITS (RELUS)

In the realm of deep learning, the choice of activation function can significantly impact the performance and training of neural networks. Among the diverse set of activation functions, Rectified Linear Units (ReLUs) have emerged as a cornerstone due to their simplicity and effectiveness.

UNDERSTANDING ACTIVATION FUNCTIONS

Before delving into the specifics of ReLUs, let's revisit the role of activation functions in neural networks. Activation functions introduce non-linearity into the network, enabling it to learn complex patterns and representations. They determine whether a neuron should be activated or not based on the weighted sum of its inputs.

Traditional activation functions like the sigmoid and hyperbolic tangent functions have been widely used. However, they suffer from limitations like the vanishing gradient problem, which hinders training in deep networks.

THE RELU ACTIVATION FUNCTION

Rectified Linear Unit (ReLU) is a breakthrough in addressing the vanishing gradient problem. It's defined as:

$$f(x) = max(0, x)$$

In simple terms, ReLU outputs the input value if it's positive, and zero otherwise. This seemingly minor change in the activation function has profound implications for deep learning.

BENEFITS OF RELUS

1. Simplicity: ReLUs are computationally efficient, requiring only a simple thresholding operation.

2. Sparse Activation: They promote sparse activations in neural networks, which means that only a subset of neurons is activated, leading to more efficient training.

3. Avoiding Vanishing Gradients: ReLUs do not saturate for positive values, preventing the vanishing gradient problem. This enables faster convergence during training.

4. Biological Plausibility: The spiking behavior of real neurons in the brain somewhat resembles ReLU activation.

LEAKY RELU AND PARAMETRIC RELU

While the traditional ReLU is a game-changer, it's not without its flaws. It can suffer from a problem called "dying ReLU," where neurons can get stuck during training, always outputting zero. To address this, two variations have been introduced:

Leaky ReLU: It allows a small, non-zero gradient when the input is negative. Mathematically, it's defined as:

$$f(x) = max(\alpha x, x)$$

Where α is a small positive constant, typically around 0.01.

Parametric ReLU (PReLU): Similar to Leaky ReLU, but α becomes a learnable parameter during training. This allows the network to adapt the slope of the negative side.

$$f(x) = max(\alpha x, x)$$

IMPLEMENTING RELUS IN NEURAL NETWORKS

Implementing ReLUs in neural networks is straightforward, thanks to the simplicity of the function. In most deep learning libraries like TensorFlow and PyTorch, ReLUs can be added as activation layers with a single line of code.

Here's an example of how to add a ReLU activation in a TensorFlow model:

```
import tensorflow as tf

model = tf.keras.Sequential([

    # Previous layers

    tf.keras.layers.Dense(64),  # Add a dense layer

    tf.keras.layers.ReLU()    # Add a ReLU activation

    # More layers

])
```

In PyTorch, it's equally straightforward:

import torch.nn as nn

model = nn.Sequential(

> *# Previous layers*

> *nn.Linear(64, 32), # Add a linear layer*

> *nn.ReLU()   # Add a ReLU activation*

> *# More layers*

)

In this section, we've explored the significance of Rectified Linear Units (ReLUs) in deep learning. Their simplicity, effectiveness, and ability to mitigate the vanishing gradient problem make them a fundamental building block in modern neural networks. In the upcoming chapters, we will continue to unravel the intricacies of deep learning, building upon this knowledge to further enhance our understanding of the A to Z of this fascinating field.

3.4. BEYOND RELUS: ADVANCED ACTIVATION FUNCTIONS**

In the realm of deep learning, activation functions play a pivotal role in shaping the behavior of neural networks. While Rectified Linear Units (ReLUs) have been a workhorse in many architectures, the landscape of activation functions extends far beyond them. In this section, we'll delve into some advanced activation functions that have proven to be invaluable for various tasks and model improvements.

3.4.1. LEAKY RELU (LRELU)

The Leaky ReLU, often denoted as LReLU, is a subtle but powerful modification of the standard ReLU. While ReLUs abruptly clip any negative input to zero, LReLUs introduce a slight slope for negative values, allowing a small gradient to flow through. This seemingly minor tweak can mitigate the "dying ReLU" problem, where neurons could become inactive during training.

Here's the mathematical formulation of the Leaky ReLU:

```
def leaky_relu(x, alpha=0.01):

    return x if x >= 0 else alpha * x
```

The `alpha` parameter controls the slope for negative values, and common values range from 0.01 to 0.3. Experimentation is often necessary to find the optimal value for your specific problem.

3.4.2. PARAMETRIC RELU (PRELU)

Parametric ReLU, or PReLU, takes the idea of Leaky ReLU a step further by making the slope trainable. Instead of using a fixed `alpha`, PReLU learns an optimal value during training, offering more flexibility. This adaptability can be particularly useful when dealing with diverse data distributions.

Here's how you can implement PReLU in a neural network using popular deep learning frameworks like PyTorch:

```
import torch

import torch.nn as nn

class PReLU(nn.Module):

    def __init__(self, num_parameters=1,
    init=0.25):

        super(PReLU, self).__init__()

        self.alpha =
nn.Parameter(torch.FloatTensor(num_param
eters).fill_(init))

    def forward(self, x):

        return torch.where(x >= 0, x, self.alpha *
x)
```

3.4.3. EXPONENTIAL LINEAR UNIT (ELU)

The Exponential Linear Unit, or ELU, offers an alternative approach to addressing the vanishing gradient problem. ELU combines the best of both worlds from ReLU and Leaky ReLU. It has a non-zero gradient for negative inputs, avoiding dead neurons, and smoothly transitions for positive inputs, which can aid convergence.

Mathematically, ELU is defined as follows:

S. Begum

```
def elu(x, alpha=1.0):

    return x if x >= 0 else alpha * (math.exp(x) -
1)
```

The `alpha` parameter controls the slope for negative values. Common values are 1.0 or smaller.

3.4.4. SWISH ACTIVATION

Swish is a relatively recent addition to the family of activation functions and has gained attention for its strong performance in various deep learning tasks. It's a smooth, non-monotonic function that tends to produce more accurate and faster converging networks.

Here's the mathematical expression for Swish:

```
def swish(x):

    return x * sigmoid(x)
```

It's worth noting that Swish introduces additional computational complexity compared to ReLU-based activations.

3.4.5. CHOOSING THE RIGHT ACTIVATION

Selecting the appropriate activation function is often a matter of experimentation and problem-specific considerations. While ReLU variants like Leaky ReLU and

A to Z of Deep Learning

Parametric ReLU are solid choices for many scenarios, the effectiveness of an activation function can vary depending on the nature of your data and the architecture of your neural network.

As you embark on your deep learning journey, remember that activation functions are just one piece of the puzzle. The interplay between activations, network architecture, and data preprocessing is what truly unlocks the potential of deep learning models. In the following chapters, we'll explore these aspects in more detail, allowing you to make informed decisions as you traverse the A to Z of deep learning.

CHAPTER 4: B FOR BACKPROPAGATION

4.1. UNRAVELING BACKPROPAGATION

In the intricate realm of deep learning, understanding the mechanics of backpropagation is akin to deciphering the engine of a powerful machine. Backpropagation, short for "backward propagation of errors," is the driving force behind the training of neural networks. This process is what allows neural networks to learn and improve their performance on a wide range of tasks, from image recognition to natural language processing.

At its core, backpropagation is a mathematical algorithm that calculates the gradient of the loss function with respect to the model's parameters. This gradient is then used to update the model's parameters in a way that reduces the error in its predictions. In simpler terms, it's the process through which a neural network learns from its mistakes and adjusts its internal parameters to make better predictions.

Let's delve into the key components of backpropagation:

Forward Pass: Before we can understand how backpropagation works, it's crucial to grasp the concept of a forward pass. During the forward pass, input data is fed into the neural network, and it travels through the layers of neurons. Each neuron performs a weighted sum of its inputs, applies an activation function, and passes the result to the next layer. This process continues until the network produces an output.

Loss Function: At the end of the forward pass, the network's output is compared to the actual target values using a loss function. The loss function quantifies how far off the network's predictions are from the true values. Common loss functions include mean squared error (MSE) for regression tasks and categorical cross-entropy for classification tasks.

Backward Pass (Backpropagation): Once the loss is computed, the magic of backpropagation begins. This phase involves calculating the gradient of the loss function with respect to each parameter in the neural network. This gradient tells us how much each parameter contributed to the error. The chain rule from calculus is employed to compute these gradients layer by layer, starting from the output layer and moving backward.

Gradient Descent: With the gradients in hand, we can now update the model's parameters to minimize the loss. Gradient descent is the most commonly used optimization algorithm for this purpose. It adjusts the parameters in the direction that reduces the loss, effectively nudging the model toward better performance.

Here's a simplified code snippet in Python to illustrate the concept of backpropagation using a hypothetical neural network:

```
# Pseudocode for Backpropagation

for epoch in range(num_epochs):
```

```
    for data_batch, target_batch in
training_data:

        # Forward Pass

        predicted_output =
neural_network(data_batch)


        # Calculate Loss

        loss = calculate_loss(predicted_output,
target_batch)


        # Backward Pass (Backpropagation)

        gradient = calculate_gradient(loss,
neural_network)

        # Update Parameters with Gradient
Descent


neural_network.update_parameters(gradient)
```

In this pseudocode, we iterate through epochs and data batches, performing forward and backward passes while updating the model's parameters using gradient descent. This is the essence of backpropagation in a neural network training process.

Backpropagation is the cornerstone of deep learning, allowing neural networks to adapt and improve their performance over time. In the subsequent sections of this chapter, we will dive deeper into the mathematics and mechanics of backpropagation, ensuring you have a solid grasp of this fundamental concept in the world of deep learning.

4.2. THE MATHEMATICS BEHIND BACKPROPAGATION

In the previous section, we introduced the concept of backpropagation as the cornerstone of training neural networks. Now, let's delve into the mathematical intricacies that power this fundamental algorithm. Understanding the mathematics behind backpropagation is essential for gaining a deep insight into how neural networks learn and adapt.

THE CHAIN RULE

At the heart of backpropagation lies the chain rule, a fundamental concept from calculus. This rule enables us to calculate the gradient of the loss function with respect to the network's weights and biases. In essence, it quantifies how much each parameter should be adjusted to minimize the error.

Mathematically, the chain rule can be expressed as follows:

$$d(f(g(x))) / dx = df/dg * dg/dx$$

In the context of neural networks, let's break down this equation:

S. Begum
- `d(f(g(x))) / dx` represents the derivative of the final loss with respect to some input `x`.
- `df/dg` represents the derivative of the loss with respect to an intermediate variable `g`.
- `dg/dx` represents the derivative of the intermediate variable `g` with respect to the input `x`.

GRADIENT DESCENT

To minimize the loss function, we utilize gradient descent, a numerical optimization technique. Gradient descent adjusts the model's weights and biases in the direction that reduces the loss. The gradient is essentially a vector of partial derivatives, and it points towards the steepest ascent of the function.

Here's a simplified version of the gradient descent update rule:

$$theta = theta - learning\_rate * gradient$$

- `theta` represents the model's weights or biases.
- `learning_rate` is a hyperparameter that controls the step size.
- `gradient` is the gradient of the loss function with respect to `theta`.

BACKPROPAGATION ALGORITHM

Now, let's see how the chain rule and gradient descent come together in the backpropagation algorithm:

A to Z of Deep Learning

1. Forward Pass: During the forward pass, we compute the output of the neural network for a given input.

2. Compute Loss: We calculate the loss between the predicted output and the actual target.

3. Backward Pass (Backpropagation): This is where the magic happens. We propagate the error backward through the network to calculate gradients for all the weights and biases.

$$delta\_output = predicted\_output - actual\_target$$

$$gradient\_weights = input\_features.T.dot(delta\_output)$$

$$gradient\_bias = delta\_output.sum()$$

4. Update Weights: Using gradient descent, we update the weights and biases to minimize the loss.

$$weights\ -=\ learning\_rate * gradient\_weights$$

$$bias\ -=\ learning\_rate * gradient\_bias$$

This iterative process continues until the model converges to a point where the loss is minimized, and the network makes accurate predictions.

Understanding the mathematics behind backpropagation equips you with the knowledge to fine-tune neural networks effectively and troubleshoot issues that may arise during training. In the next section, we'll explore advanced techniques that enhance the training process and make deep learning models even more powerful.

4.3. OPTIMIZING NEURAL NETWORKS

Optimizing neural networks is a pivotal step in the deep learning process. While backpropagation helps us adjust the weights and biases of our network to minimize errors, optimization algorithms determine how these adjustments are made. These algorithms play a crucial role in ensuring that our neural network converges to a solution efficiently and effectively.

GRADIENT DESCENT

One of the fundamental optimization techniques in deep learning is Gradient Descent. At its core, Gradient Descent is an iterative algorithm used to minimize a cost function. It works by adjusting the model's parameters (weights and biases) in the direction that reduces the cost, ultimately converging towards an optimal solution.

Let's implement a simple gradient descent algorithm in Python:

```
# Define the cost function

def cost_function(parameters):
```

```
        # Calculate the cost based on your neural
    network's performance

        # This could be mean squared error or cross-
    entropy loss, depending on your task

        # Return the cost

    # Initialize the parameters (weights and
    biases) randomly

    parameters = initialize_parameters()

    # Set the learning rate

    learning_rate = 0.01

    # Define the number of iterations

    num_iterations = 1000

    # Gradient Descent

    for i in range(num_iterations):

        # Calculate the gradient of the cost function
        with respect to parameters

        gradient =
        calculate_gradient(cost_function,
        parameters)

        # Update the parameters using the gradient
        and learning rate
```

```
    parameters =
update_parameters(parameters, gradient,
learning_rate)

# Your neural network's parameters are now
optimized
```

This code snippet illustrates a simplified Gradient Descent implementation. In practice, libraries like TensorFlow and PyTorch provide optimized functions for gradient descent, making it more efficient and convenient for deep learning tasks.

OTHER OPTIMIZATION ALGORITHMS

Gradient Descent is just the tip of the iceberg when it comes to optimization algorithms. Researchers and practitioners have developed various advanced optimization techniques like Adam, RMSprop, and Adagrad, which have proven to be highly effective in training deep neural networks.

In this chapter, we've explored the significance of optimizing neural networks, with a focus on Gradient Descent as a foundational technique. As you progress in your deep learning journey, you'll encounter and experiment with a variety of optimization algorithms, each with its strengths and use cases. These tools will empower you to tackle increasingly complex problems and unlock the full potential of deep learning.

In the next chapter, we'll explore the fascinating world of Convolutional Neural Networks (CNNs) and their applications in computer vision.

CHAPTER 5: C FOR CONVOLUTIONAL NEURAL NETWORKS (CNNS)

5.1. THE BASICS OF CONVOLUTION

In the realm of deep learning, Convolutional Neural Networks, or CNNs, stand as the bedrock of image and pattern recognition tasks. These neural networks, inspired by the human visual system, have revolutionized computer vision and extended their reach to various domains, including medical imaging, autonomous vehicles, and more.

At the heart of CNNs lies the operation of convolution, a fundamental mathematical concept that underpins their effectiveness. Convolutional layers in these networks play a pivotal role in detecting features within an image, such as edges, corners, and textures, by systematically scanning through the input data. This process enables CNNs to learn hierarchical representations of visual information, from simple shapes to complex structures.

Let's delve into the basics of convolution and see how it forms the building block of CNNs.

UNDERSTANDING CONVOLUTION

Convolution is a mathematical operation that combines two functions to produce a third. In the context of CNNs, one function represents the input data (e.g., an image), and the other is known as the kernel or filter. The convolution operation involves sliding the kernel over the input data and computing the element-wise multiplication between the kernel and the corresponding region of the input. The results are then summed up to form a single output value.

Mathematically, the 2D convolution operation can be defined as follows:

$$output[i, j] = sum(sum(input\_slice * kernel))$$

Here, `output[i, j]` is the value at position `(i, j)` in the output feature map, `input_slice` corresponds to the region of the input data that aligns with the kernel, and `kernel` is the convolutional filter.

CONVOLUTION IN ACTION

Let's illustrate the concept of convolution with a simple example. Consider a grayscale image of size 5x5 and a 3x3 kernel:

Image:

1 1 1 0 0

0 1 1 1 0

0 0 1 1 1

0 0 1 1 0

0 1 1 0 0

Kernel:

101

010

101

To compute the output at the top-left corner of the feature map (position `[0, 0]`), we perform the following element-wise multiplication and summation:

$$output[0, 0] = sum(sum(input[0:3, 0:3] * kernel)) = sum(sum([[1, 0, 1], [0, 1, 1], [0, 0, 1]] * [[1, 0, 1], [0, 1, 0], [1, 0, 1]])) = 5$$

This result becomes the top-left value in the output feature map. The process repeats by sliding the kernel across the entire image, producing a feature map that captures the presence of certain features within the image.

In the subsequent sections of this chapter, we will explore how CNNs utilize convolutional layers for feature extraction and the architecture of these networks for image recognition tasks. Convolution is just the beginning of the fascinating journey through the world of Convolutional Neural Networks.

5.2. BUILDING BLOCKS OF CNNS

In the previous section, we introduced the basics of Convolutional Neural Networks (CNNs) and their pivotal role in computer vision tasks. Now, it's time to delve deeper into the architectural elements that make CNNs so effective. CNNs are renowned for their ability to automatically learn hierarchical features from data, thanks to their distinctive building blocks. Let's explore these key components:

5.2.1. CONVOLUTIONAL LAYERS

At the heart of CNNs lie the convolutional layers. These layers apply convolutional operations to input data. Think of convolution as a sliding window that scans the input image to detect patterns. Each convolutional operation involves a kernel, which is a small filter matrix. The kernel convolves across the input, performing element-wise multiplications and summing the results to produce a feature map.

Here's a simplified example in Python using TensorFlow:

```python
import tensorflow as tf

# Create a Conv2D layer

conv_layer = tf.keras.layers.Conv2D(
    filters=64,          # Number of filters
    kernel_size=(3, 3),   # Kernel size (3x3)
    activation='relu',    # Activation function
    input_shape=(28, 28, 1) # Input shape (e.g.,
    for 28x28 grayscale images)
```

```
)

# Apply the convolutional layer to an input
tensor

output = conv_layer(input_tensor)
```

5.2.2. POOLING LAYERS

Pooling layers are another crucial component. They reduce the spatial dimensions of the feature maps, effectively downsampling the information. The most common pooling operation is max-pooling, which retains the maximum value within a fixed window and discards the rest.

Here's how you can add max-pooling to your CNN using TensorFlow:

```
# Create a MaxPooling2D layer

pooling_layer =
tf.keras.layers.MaxPooling2D(

   pool_size=(2, 2) # Pooling window size
(2x2)

)

# Apply the pooling layer to a feature map

output = pooling_layer(feature_map)
```

5.2.3. FULLY CONNECTED LAYERS

After several convolutional and pooling layers, CNNs often incorporate fully connected layers to perform classification or regression tasks. These layers connect every neuron to every neuron in the previous and subsequent layers.

Here's a snippet illustrating fully connected layers in Keras:

```
# Create a Dense (fully connected) layer

dense_layer = tf.keras.layers.Dense(

    units=128,    # Number of neurons in the layer

    activation='relu' # Activation function

)

# Apply the dense layer to a flattened input
(e.g., output from previous layers)

output = dense_layer(flattened_input)
```

5.2.4. ACTIVATION FUNCTIONS

Activation functions are applied to introduce non-linearity into the network. ReLU (Rectified Linear Unit) is one of the most popular choices because it effectively handles vanishing gradient problems.

```
# Apply ReLU activation to a layer's output

output = tf.keras.layers.ReLU()(input)
```

In this section, we've uncovered the foundational elements of Convolutional Neural Networks, paving the way for a deeper understanding of their capabilities in computer vision applications. In the next section, we'll explore practical applications and best practices for designing CNN architectures to tackle real-world problems.

5.3. APPLICATIONS OF CNNS IN COMPUTER VISION

In the previous sections of this chapter, we've delved into the mechanics of Convolutional Neural Networks (CNNs), dissecting their architecture and understanding their core principles. Now, we turn our attention to the exciting realm of applications, where CNNs truly shine, particularly in the field of Computer Vision.

5.3.1. IMAGE CLASSIFICATION

One of the fundamental applications of CNNs in Computer Vision is image classification. CNNs excel at categorizing images into predefined classes or labels. Let's look at a code snippet to illustrate how to build a simple image classifier using Python and popular deep learning libraries such as TensorFlow and Keras:

```
import tensorflow as tf

from tensorflow.keras import layers, models
```

S. Begum

```python
# Define a Sequential model

model = models.Sequential()

# Add convolutional layers

model.add(layers.Conv2D(32, (3, 3),
activation='relu', input_shape=(64, 64, 3)))

model.add(layers.MaxPooling2D((2, 2)))

model.add(layers.Conv2D(64, (3, 3),
activation='relu'))

model.add(layers.MaxPooling2D((2, 2)))

model.add(layers.Conv2D(128, (3, 3),
activation='relu'))

model.add(layers.MaxPooling2D((2, 2)))

# Flatten the output and add fully connected
layers

model.add(layers.Flatten())

model.add(layers.Dense(128,
activation='relu'))

model.add(layers.Dense(10,
activation='softmax'))

# Compile the model

model.compile(optimizer='adam',

        loss='sparse_categorical_crossentropy',
```

$$metrics=['accuracy'])$$

Train the model with your dataset

This code outlines the construction of a CNN-based image classifier. The network comprises convolutional layers followed by max-pooling layers to extract essential features from the input images, which are then fed into densely connected layers for classification.

5.3.2. OBJECT DETECTION

CNNs have revolutionized object detection in images and videos. They enable the identification and localization of objects within an image, often referred to as bounding box detection. One of the groundbreaking architectures for object detection is the Region-based Convolutional Neural Network (R-CNN) family, including Faster R-CNN and Mask R-CNN. These models can identify and segment objects in an image.

5.3.3. FACIAL RECOGNITION

Facial recognition systems, used for various applications such as unlocking smartphones or enhancing security, frequently rely on CNNs. These networks can learn intricate facial features and match them to known individuals. A popular dataset used for facial recognition is the LFW (Labeled Faces in the Wild) dataset, which contains a vast collection of images of celebrities.

5.3.4. AUTONOMOUS VEHICLES

In the realm of autonomous vehicles, CNNs play a pivotal role. They are used for tasks like lane detection, traffic sign recognition, and object detection. These applications enable self-driving cars to navigate safely through complex environments, making them reliant on deep learning technology.

5.3.5. MEDICAL IMAGE ANALYSIS

CNNs are invaluable in the field of medical image analysis. They assist in tasks like tumor detection in MRI scans, classifying skin lesions, and identifying abnormalities in X-rays. CNNs can learn to identify subtle patterns and anomalies that might elude human eyes.

In this chapter, we've barely scratched the surface of the myriad applications of CNNs in Computer Vision. From image classification to object detection, facial recognition to autonomous vehicles, and medical image analysis, the versatility of CNNs continues to drive innovation across various domains, reshaping the way we interact with visual data. As you explore further, you'll discover the limitless potential of Convolutional Neural Networks in unlocking the depths of intelligence in the world of Computer Vision.

CHAPTER 6: D FOR DEEP LEARNING FRAMEWORKS

6.1. INTRODUCTION TO DEEP LEARNING FRAMEWORKS

In the ever-evolving landscape of deep learning, the choice of the right tools can make all the difference. Deep learning frameworks are the scaffolding upon which we build our neural networks and harness the power of artificial intelligence. In this chapter, we embark on a journey to explore the fundamental aspects of deep learning frameworks.

Deep learning frameworks provide a bridge between the abstract mathematical concepts of neural networks and their practical implementation. They offer a structured environment where you can design, train, and deploy your deep learning models efficiently. These frameworks come equipped with a plethora of pre-built functions, optimization techniques, and tools to simplify the complex task of creating and training neural networks.

Two heavyweight contenders dominate the landscape: TensorFlow and PyTorch. Let's briefly introduce each of them:

TensorFlow: Developed by Google Brain, TensorFlow is one of the most popular and widely used deep learning frameworks. It is renowned for its flexibility and scalability, making it an ideal choice for both research and production applications. TensorFlow's high-level API,

Keras, provides a user-friendly interface for building neural networks with minimal code.

```
# Example TensorFlow code snippet

import tensorflow as tf

# Create a simple neural network using Keras

model = tf.keras.Sequential([

    tf.keras.layers.Dense(128, activation='relu',
input_shape=(784,)),

    tf.keras.layers.Dropout(0.2),

    tf.keras.layers.Dense(10,
activation='softmax')

])

# Compile the model

model.compile(optimizer='adam',

        loss='sparse_categorical_crossentropy',

        metrics=['accuracy'])
```

PyTorch: Developed by Facebook's AI Research lab (FAIR), PyTorch has gained immense popularity in the deep learning community. It is favored for its dynamic computation graph, which allows for more intuitive model construction and debugging. PyTorch is often the choice of researchers due to its ease of use.

A to Z of Deep Learning

```python
# Example PyTorch code snippet

import torch

import torch.nn as nn

import torch.optim as optim


# Define a simple neural network
class Net(nn.Module):
    def __init__(self):
        super(Net, self).__init__()
        self.fc1 = nn.Linear(784, 128)
        self.fc2 = nn.Linear(128, 10)
    def forward(self, x):
        x = torch.relu(self.fc1(x))
        x = torch.softmax(self.fc2(x), dim=1)
        return x
# Create an instance of the network
model = Net()
# Define the loss function and optimizer
criterion = nn.CrossEntropyLoss()
```

```
optimizer = optim.Adam(model.parameters(),
lr=0.001)
```

In the upcoming sections, we will delve deeper into both TensorFlow and PyTorch, exploring their features, advantages, and use cases. By the end of this chapter, you will have a solid understanding of these frameworks and be well-equipped to choose the one that best suits your deep learning endeavors. Whether you're a researcher pushing the boundaries of AI or a developer implementing practical solutions, the choice of framework plays a pivotal role in your journey through deep learning.

6.2. TENSORFLOW: GOOGLE'S POWERHOUSE

In the realm of deep learning frameworks, TensorFlow stands as a true juggernaut. Developed by Google, it has grown to become one of the most influential and widely adopted tools in the field. Its versatility, scalability, and extensive community support make it a powerhouse for deep learning research and application.

TensorFlow is an open-source machine learning framework that offers a range of tools and libraries for building various machine learning and deep learning models. Here, we'll delve into why TensorFlow has gained such prominence and explore some of its key features.

WHY TENSORFLOW?

TensorFlow's popularity can be attributed to several factors:

A to Z of Deep Learning

1. Flexibility: TensorFlow provides a flexible ecosystem for developing and deploying machine learning models. It supports both traditional machine learning and deep learning, allowing you to seamlessly transition between the two.

2. Scalability: Whether you're running models on a single machine or a distributed cluster, TensorFlow scales effortlessly. This makes it suitable for both small-scale experiments and large-scale production systems.

3. Community and Ecosystem: TensorFlow boasts a vast and active community of developers and researchers. This has led to an extensive ecosystem of pre-built models, tools, and resources, which can significantly accelerate your deep learning projects.

4. TensorBoard: TensorBoard, an integrated visualization tool, simplifies model debugging and monitoring. It helps you visualize metrics, explore model graphs, and track training progress.

5. TensorFlow Serving: For deploying models in real-world applications, TensorFlow Serving offers a production-ready solution. It ensures that your models are easily accessible via APIs, making it ideal for applications like recommendation systems and image recognition.

6. TensorFlow.js: TensorFlow's versatility extends to the web. TensorFlow.js allows you to run machine learning models directly in web browsers, opening up possibilities for browser-based applications.

S. Begum

GETTING STARTED WITH TENSORFLOW

Let's dip our toes into TensorFlow with a simple example. In this snippet, we'll showcase how to create a basic neural network using TensorFlow's high-level API, Keras. If you haven't already installed TensorFlow, you can do so via pip:

pip install tensorflow

Now, let's create a neural network for image classification:

import tensorflow as tf

from tensorflow import keras

 # Load a dataset (e.g., Fashion MNIST)

(x_train, y_train), (x_test, y_test) = keras.datasets.fashion_mnist.load_data()

 # Preprocess the data

x_train, x_test = x_train / 255.0, x_test / 255.0

 # Build a simple neural network model

model = keras.Sequential([

  keras.layers.Flatten(input_shape=(28, 28)),

  keras.layers.Dense(128, activation='relu'),

  keras.layers.Dropout(0.2),

```
        keras.layers.Dense(10)

])

# Compile the model

model.compile(optimizer='adam',


loss=tf.keras.losses.SparseCategoricalCrossent
ropy(from_logits=True),

        metrics=['accuracy'])

# Train the model

model.fit(x_train, y_train, epochs=5)

# Evaluate the model

test_loss, test_acc = model.evaluate(x_test,
y_test, verbose=2)

print(f'\nTest accuracy: {test_acc}')
```

This simple example demonstrates how TensorFlow, in conjunction with Keras, allows you to build, train, and evaluate neural networks with ease. As we continue our journey through deep learning, we'll explore more advanced topics and techniques using TensorFlow, enabling you to harness its full potential in your projects.

EXPLORING TENSORFLOW'S LAYERS

In TensorFlow, building deep neural networks is made more accessible by the concept of layers. Each layer in a model performs specific operations on the data it receives. We've already seen the use of layers in our previous example. Here, we'll delve a bit deeper.

TensorFlow provides a wide array of layers to design your neural network architecture. Here are some common layers and their roles:

- Dense Layer: Also known as a fully connected layer, it connects every neuron in one layer to every neuron in the next layer. It's often used in the output layer for classification tasks.

- Convolutional Layer (Conv2D): Essential for image processing, this layer performs convolutions on input data, capturing patterns and features within the data.

- Pooling Layer (MaxPooling2D, AveragePooling2D): These layers reduce the spatial dimensions of the data, helping to decrease the computational load and retain essential information.

- Recurrent Layer (LSTM, GRU): These layers are crucial for sequential data, such as natural language processing or time series analysis. They enable models to capture temporal dependencies.

- Dropout Layer: Dropout layers help prevent overfitting by randomly deactivating a fraction of neurons during training.

- Batch Normalization Layer: This layer helps stabilize and accelerate training by normalizing input values to each layer.

A to Z of Deep Learning
ADVANCED FEATURES

As you progress in your deep learning journey, you'll discover advanced features in TensorFlow that empower you to tackle complex tasks:

- Custom Layers and Models: TensorFlow allows you to create custom layers and models tailored to your specific needs. This flexibility is invaluable for experimental architectures.

- Transfer Learning: Leveraging pre-trained models, such as those from the TensorFlow Hub or the TensorFlow Model Garden, can save you significant time and resources when working on tasks like image recognition.

- Distributed Training: For large-scale deep learning tasks, TensorFlow provides tools for distributed training across multiple GPUs or even multiple machines.

- TensorFlow Extended (TFX): If you're working on machine learning pipelines and productionizing models, TFX offers a comprehensive suite of tools for managing the end-to-end machine learning lifecycle.

In this chapter, we've only scratched the surface of what TensorFlow has to offer. As we journey through the A to Z of deep learning, we'll explore more advanced topics, including reinforcement learning, generative adversarial networks (GANs), and natural language processing, all with TensorFlow as our trusty companion.

So, whether you're just starting your deep learning adventure or you're a seasoned practitioner, TensorFlow's capabilities and community support make it a formidable choice for your machine learning endeavors. Get ready to unlock the depths of intelligence with TensorFlow as your guide.

6.3. PYTORCH: THE PREFERRED CHOICE OF RESEARCHERS

In the realm of deep learning frameworks, PyTorch has emerged as a shining star, capturing the hearts and minds of researchers and developers alike. Renowned for its flexibility, dynamic computation graph, and Pythonic approach, PyTorch has become the preferred choice for those pushing the boundaries of artificial intelligence.

WHY PYTORCH?

PyTorch's popularity can be attributed to several key factors:

1. Dynamic Computation Graph: Unlike some other frameworks, PyTorch utilizes a dynamic computation graph. This means that the graph is built on-the-fly as operations are executed. For researchers, this dynamic nature allows for more intuitive and flexible model development. You can change the network architecture, modify parameters, and debug with ease.

2. Pythonic Design: PyTorch was designed with Python developers in mind. If you're already comfortable with Python, you'll find PyTorch's syntax and debugging tools to be highly accessible. This lowers the learning curve and accelerates development.

3. Community and Ecosystem: PyTorch boasts a vibrant and rapidly growing community. This translates into extensive documentation, a wealth of pre-built models, and a wide range of third-party extensions and libraries. You're never alone when working with PyTorch.

INSTALLING PYTORCH

Before diving into PyTorch, you'll need to install it. The preferred way is through pip, Python's package manager. Depending on your system and whether you need GPU support, the installation commands may vary:

```
# For CPU-only support, use this command

pip install torch
```

```
# For GPU support (assuming you have a
compatible GPU)

pip install torch torchvision torchaudio -f
https://download.pytorch.org/whl/cuXXX/to
rch_stable.html
```

Replace `cuXXX` with your specific CUDA version if you're using GPU acceleration.

A SIMPLE PYTORCH EXAMPLE

Let's create a basic PyTorch example to get you started. We'll build a small neural network that classifies

S. Begum

handwritten digits using the famous MNIST dataset. This example demonstrates PyTorch's simplicity and elegance.

```python
import torch

import torch.nn as nn

import torch.optim as optim

import torchvision

import torchvision.transforms as transforms


# Define a simple neural network
class Net(nn.Module):
  def __init__(self):
    super(Net, self).__init__()
    self.fc1 = nn.Linear(28 * 28, 128)
    self.fc2 = nn.Linear(128, 10)
  def forward(self, x):
    x = torch.flatten(x, 1) # Flatten input
    x = torch.relu(self.fc1(x))
    x = self.fc2(x)
    return x
```

A to Z of Deep Learning

```python
# Load and preprocess the dataset

transform =
transforms.Compose([transforms.ToTensor(),
transforms.Normalize((0.5,), (0.5,))])

trainset =
torchvision.datasets.MNIST(root='./data',
train=True, download=True,
transform=transform)

trainloader =
torch.utils.data.DataLoader(trainset,
batch_size=4, shuffle=True)

# Create the neural network, loss function,
and optimizer

net = Net()

criterion = nn.CrossEntropyLoss()

optimizer = optim.SGD(net.parameters(),
lr=0.001, momentum=0.9)

# Training loop

for epoch in range(5):  # Loop over the dataset
multiple times

    running_loss = 0.0

    for i, data in enumerate(trainloader, 0):

        inputs, labels = data

        # Zero the parameter gradients
```

```
optimizer.zero_grad()

# Forward + backward + optimize

outputs = net(inputs)

loss = criterion(outputs, labels)

loss.backward()

optimizer.step()

# Print statistics

running_loss += loss.item()

if i % 2000 == 1999: # Print every 2000 mini-batches

    print(f'[{epoch + 1}, {i + 1:5d}] loss: {running_loss / 2000:.3f}')

    running_loss = 0.0

print('Finished Training')
```

This code represents a basic PyTorch workflow for training a neural network. It's just the tip of the iceberg, but it showcases PyTorch's simplicity and power. In the chapters to come, we'll dive deeper into PyTorch, exploring advanced concepts and real-world applications. PyTorch's flexibility will empower you to tackle a wide range of deep learning challenges with confidence.

CHAPTER 7: E FOR ETHICS IN DEEP LEARNING

7.1. THE ETHICAL LANDSCAPE OF DEEP LEARNING

In the ever-expanding realm of deep learning, technological advancements and the proliferation of artificial intelligence applications have opened new frontiers. However, with great power comes great responsibility. The ethical considerations surrounding deep learning are more crucial than ever before. In this chapter, we delve into the complex and evolving ethical landscape of deep learning, exploring the challenges, dilemmas, and potential solutions that arise in this fast-paced field.

UNDERSTANDING ETHICAL DILEMMAS

Before we embark on this exploration, it's essential to grasp the ethical dilemmas posed by deep learning. At its core, deep learning involves the development of algorithms and models that can make decisions, predictions, and classifications autonomously. These systems, often referred to as neural networks, can learn from vast datasets and generalize patterns, which is both their strength and vulnerability.

Imagine a self-driving car that relies on deep learning to make split-second decisions on the road. Should it prioritize the safety of the occupants, pedestrians, or both? This is just one of many ethical questions that arise. Some other common dilemmas include:

S. Begum

- Bias and Fairness: Deep learning models can inadvertently perpetuate biases present in their training data, leading to unfair or discriminatory outcomes.

- Privacy Concerns: The collection and analysis of vast amounts of data can infringe on individuals' privacy, raising questions about consent and data protection.

- Transparency and Accountability: Deep learning models are often seen as "black boxes" due to their complexity, making it challenging to understand how they arrive at specific decisions and who is responsible when things go wrong.

ADDRESSING ETHICAL CONCERNS

Deep learning practitioners and researchers are acutely aware of these ethical concerns and are actively working to address them. Here are some approaches being taken to navigate the ethical landscape:

1. Fairness-aware Algorithms: Researchers are developing algorithms that can detect and mitigate biases in data and model predictions, ensuring that AI systems make fair decisions.

2. Privacy-Preserving Techniques: Techniques like federated learning and differential privacy are being used to protect individual data while still enabling model training on distributed datasets.

3. Ethical Guidelines and Frameworks: Organizations and institutions are creating ethical guidelines and frameworks

to provide a roadmap for ethical AI development and deployment.

4. Transparency and Explainability: Efforts are underway to make deep learning models more transparent and interpretable, allowing users to understand how and why a decision was made.

In this chapter, we will dive deeper into each of these aspects, exploring real-world examples and case studies that shed light on the ethical complexities of deep learning. Our goal is to equip you with a comprehensive understanding of the ethical landscape, empowering you to make informed decisions and contribute to the responsible development of deep learning technologies.

7.2. BIAS AND FAIRNESS IN AI

In the realm of artificial intelligence, the issues of bias and fairness hold profound significance. As AI systems increasingly permeate various aspects of our lives, from lending decisions to hiring processes and even criminal justice, ensuring fairness and mitigating bias is of paramount importance. In this chapter, we will delve into the complexities surrounding bias and fairness in AI, shedding light on the challenges and solutions in this crucial area.

UNDERSTANDING BIAS IN AI

Bias in AI refers to the presence of systematic and unfair discrimination in the outcomes produced by machine learning algorithms. This bias can emerge from various sources, including biased training data, biased model design, and biased decision-making processes.

Biased Training Data: Machine learning models learn from historical data, and if this data contains biases, the model may learn and perpetuate those biases. For example, if a hiring dataset contains a historical bias toward hiring more men than women, an AI system trained on this data may unfairly favor male candidates in future hiring decisions.

Biased Model Design: Bias can also be introduced through the design of the model itself. The features and attributes selected for training, as well as the algorithm chosen, can unintentionally amplify existing biases.

THE IMPORTANCE OF FAIRNESS

Fairness in AI is the pursuit of ensuring that the decisions and predictions made by AI systems are equitable and just. Fairness is not a one-size-fits-all concept and can vary depending on the context and domain in which AI is applied.

For instance, in the context of lending decisions, fairness may involve ensuring that loan approval rates are similar across different demographic groups, such as race or gender. In the criminal justice system, fairness might mean that AI algorithms used for risk assessment do not disproportionately label one group as high-risk compared to another.

ADDRESSING BIAS AND PROMOTING FAIRNESS

Mitigating bias and promoting fairness in AI is an ongoing challenge that requires a multi-faceted approach. Here are some key strategies:

1. Data Preprocessing: Careful preprocessing of training data can help reduce bias. This may involve removing biased attributes, oversampling underrepresented groups, or generating synthetic data.

2. Algorithmic Fairness: Researchers are developing algorithms that are explicitly designed to be fair. These algorithms aim to minimize discrimination and bias in their predictions.

3. Transparency and Explainability: Understanding how AI systems make decisions is crucial for identifying and rectifying bias. Tools for model interpretability can shed light on the decision-making process.

4. Diverse Stakeholder Involvement: Ensuring diverse perspectives in the development and deployment of AI systems can help uncover and rectify biases that might otherwise go unnoticed.

5. Regulations and Standards: Governments and industry bodies are increasingly recognizing the need for regulations and standards to address bias and fairness in AI.

```
# Example of bias mitigation in a gender-
based hiring model

import pandas as pd
```

S. Begum

```python
from sklearn.preprocessing import
LabelEncoder

from sklearn.model_selection import
train_test_split

from sklearn.ensemble import
RandomForestClassifier

from sklearn.metrics import accuracy_score,
classification_report

# Load and preprocess the dataset

data = pd.read_csv("hiring_data.csv")

data['gender'] =
LabelEncoder().fit_transform(data['gender'])

X = data.drop('hired', axis=1)

y = data['hired']

# Split the data into training and testing sets

X_train, X_test, y_train, y_test =
train_test_split(X, y, test_size=0.2,
random_state=42)

# Train a random forest classifier

clf =
RandomForestClassifier(n_estimators=100,
random_state=42)

clf.fit(X_train, y_train)
```

```
# Make predictions on the test data

y_pred = clf.predict(X_test)

# Evaluate the model

accuracy = accuracy_score(y_test, y_pred)

report = classification_report(y_test, y_pred)

print("Model Accuracy:", accuracy)

print("Classification Report:\n", report)
```

In this code snippet, we see an example of a gender-based hiring model. It's essential to monitor and evaluate such models for bias and fairness, as discussed in this chapter.

In the rapidly evolving landscape of AI, addressing bias and promoting fairness is an ongoing journey that requires collaboration, vigilance, and a commitment to ethical AI practices.

7.3. PRIVACY AND SECURITY CONCERNS

In our journey through the world of deep learning, it is essential to pause and reflect on the ethical dimensions that surround this transformative technology. Among these considerations, privacy and security stand as paramount concerns. In this section, we will delve into the intricacies of safeguarding data and protecting the privacy of individuals in the era of deep learning.

S. Begum

PRIVACY IN THE AGE OF DEEP LEARNING

Deep learning models thrive on data—massive amounts of it. This data often includes sensitive information about individuals, ranging from personal messages to medical records. As such, the responsible use of data in deep learning is not merely a technical concern; it is a moral and legal imperative.

Legal Frameworks: Several countries have enacted data protection laws, such as the General Data Protection Regulation (GDPR) in the European Union and the California Consumer Privacy Act (CCPA) in the United States. These laws mandate transparency in data collection, consent from individuals, and the right to be forgotten.

Data Minimization: One approach to protect privacy is data minimization—collecting and retaining only the minimum amount of data necessary for the intended purpose. This reduces the risk of data breaches and unauthorized access.

SECURITY CHALLENGES IN DEEP LEARNING

Deep learning systems, like any other technology, are susceptible to security vulnerabilities. These vulnerabilities can have far-reaching consequences, from the compromise of sensitive data to the manipulation of deep learning models.

Adversarial Attacks: Adversarial attacks involve intentionally manipulating input data to trick a deep learning model. For instance, an image classifier can be deceived into misclassifying an image with imperceptible alterations.

Model Vulnerabilities: Deep learning models can be susceptible to exploitation through techniques like model inversion, where attackers attempt to reconstruct sensitive data from the model's outputs.

PROTECTING PRIVACY AND ENHANCING SECURITY

As a practitioner in the field of deep learning, it is vital to adopt measures that protect privacy and enhance security. Here are some key steps you can take:

1. Data Anonymization: Remove personally identifiable information (PII) from datasets to ensure that even if the data is breached, individuals cannot be identified.

2. Federated Learning: Implement federated learning, a technique where models are trained on decentralized data, ensuring data never leaves the user's device. Google's Federated Learning of Cohorts (FLoC) is an example of privacy-preserving techniques.

3. Regular Model Audits: Continuously audit your deep learning models for vulnerabilities and evaluate their robustness against adversarial attacks.

4. Secure Data Handling: Employ strong encryption techniques and secure data transmission protocols to protect data at rest and in transit.

 # Example of data anonymization using Python

S. Begum

```python
def anonymize_data(data):

    for record in data:

        record['name'] = 'John Doe'

        record['email'] = 'johndoe@example.com'

    return data
```

As we navigate the ever-evolving landscape of deep learning, let us do so with a profound sense of responsibility. By addressing privacy and security concerns proactively, we can ensure that this remarkable technology continues to benefit society while respecting individual rights and data security.

CHAPTER 8: F FOR FUTURE TRENDS IN DEEP LEARNING

8.1. EMERGING TRENDS AND TECHNOLOGIES

As we journey deeper into the realm of deep learning, it's essential to keep our eyes on the horizon and anticipate the exciting developments that lie ahead. The field of deep learning is dynamic and ever-evolving, with new trends and technologies emerging at a rapid pace. In this chapter, we'll explore some of the most prominent emerging trends that are shaping the future of deep learning.

8.1.1. TRANSFORMERS: REVOLUTIONIZING NATURAL LANGUAGE PROCESSING

One of the most significant breakthroughs in recent years is the rise of transformer models. Transformers have revolutionized natural language processing (NLP) and opened up new possibilities for understanding and generating human language. The introduction of models like BERT (Bidirectional Encoder Representations from Transformers) and GPT (Generative Pre-trained Transformer) has led to remarkable advances in tasks such as language translation, sentiment analysis, and text generation.

Let's take a closer look at the code snippet for using a pre-trained transformer model for text generation:

```
import torch
```

S. Begum

```python
from transformers import
GPT2LMHeadModel, GPT2Tokenizer

# Load pre-trained GPT-2 model and tokenizer

model_name = "gpt2-medium"

tokenizer =
GPT2Tokenizer.from_pretrained(model_name
)

model =
GPT2LMHeadModel.from_pretrained(model_
name)

# Generate text using the model

input_text = "Once upon a time"

input_ids = tokenizer.encode(input_text,
return_tensors="pt")

output = model.generate(input_ids,
max_length=50, num_return_sequences=1,
no_repeat_ngram_size=2, top_p=0.92)

# Decode and print the generated text

generated_text = tokenizer.decode(output[0],
skip_special_tokens=True)

print(generated_text)
```

8.1.2. FEDERATED LEARNING: PRIVACY-PRESERVING AI

Privacy concerns have become increasingly prominent in the era of deep learning. Federated learning has emerged as a promising solution to address these concerns while still making advancements in AI. With federated learning, models are trained on decentralized data sources without sharing the raw data. This approach has applications in healthcare, finance, and other sensitive domains.

Here's a high-level code snippet illustrating the concept of federated learning:

```
# Federated learning pseudocode

for each client in the network:

    local_model = initialize_model()

    local_data = client.get_local_data()

    local_model.train(local_data)

    client.send_local_update(local_model)

    global_model = aggregate_local_updates()
```

8.1.3. EXPLAINABLE AI (XAI): INTERPRETABLE MODELS

As AI systems become more integrated into our lives, the need for transparency and interpretability has grown.

S. Begum

Explainable AI (XAI) focuses on developing models that can provide meaningful explanations for their decisions. Techniques such as LIME (Local Interpretable Model-agnostic Explanations) and SHAP (SHapley Additive exPlanations) are gaining traction in the quest for interpretable AI.

Here's an example of using SHAP to explain a model's predictions:

```
import shap

import xgboost

# Load a pre-trained XGBoost model

model = xgboost.XGBClassifier()

model.load_model("xgboost_model.model")

# Create an explainer using SHAP

explainer = shap.Explainer(model)

shap_values = explainer.shap_values(X_test)

# Visualize the feature importance

shap.summary_plot(shap_values, X_test,
feature_names=feature_names)
```

These are just a few glimpses of the fascinating trends and technologies shaping the future of deep learning. As you delve deeper into this chapter, you'll gain a more comprehensive understanding of how these innovations are propelling the field forward and how you can be a part of this ever-evolving journey.

8.2. QUANTUM COMPUTING AND DEEP LEARNING

In our exploration of the A to Z of deep learning, we've delved into the remarkable advancements and capabilities of traditional computing systems. However, as we advance further into the 21st century, another revolutionary technology is on the horizon - quantum computing. Quantum computing is poised to disrupt the landscape of computing as we know it, and its implications for deep learning are nothing short of profound.

UNDERSTANDING QUANTUM COMPUTING

At its core, quantum computing leverages the principles of quantum mechanics to perform computations that are exponentially faster than classical computers for certain types of problems. Classical computers, including the most powerful supercomputers, rely on bits, which can represent information as either a 0 or a 1. Quantum computers, on the other hand, utilize quantum bits or qubits. Unlike classical bits, qubits can exist in multiple states simultaneously, thanks to a phenomenon called superposition.

Superposition enables quantum computers to explore multiple solutions to a problem in parallel. This unique capability holds the potential to revolutionize deep learning by dramatically speeding up complex calculations, such as training deep neural networks and optimizing algorithms.

S. Begum

QUANTUM MACHINE LEARNING

Quantum machine learning (QML) is a burgeoning field that seeks to harness the power of quantum computing for various machine learning tasks, including deep learning. One of the most promising applications of QML is in solving optimization problems, which are fundamental to training neural networks.

Quantum computers can search through vast solution spaces more efficiently than classical computers, making them ideal for finding the optimal parameters of deep learning models. This can lead to significantly faster training times and more accurate models.

CHALLENGES AND CONSIDERATIONS

While the potential of quantum computing in deep learning is exciting, several challenges and considerations must be addressed. Quantum computers are still in their infancy, and large-scale, fault-tolerant quantum computers capable of outperforming classical computers in deep learning tasks are not yet widely available.

Additionally, integrating quantum computing into existing deep learning frameworks and algorithms is a complex endeavor. Researchers are actively working on developing quantum algorithms and tools that can seamlessly interface with classical deep learning pipelines.

A GLIMPSE INTO THE FUTURE

As quantum computing technology matures, it is likely to become an integral part of the deep learning landscape.

Researchers and practitioners in the field of deep learning will need to stay abreast of developments in quantum computing and explore how this quantum leap in computation power can be harnessed to unlock new frontiers in artificial intelligence.

In the next chapter, we will conclude our journey through the A to Z of deep learning, reflecting on our exploration and looking ahead to the ever-evolving world of artificial intelligence.

Stay curious, for the future of deep learning is poised to be both quantum and exciting.

8.3. THE FUTURE OF ARTIFICIAL INTELLIGENCE

As we journey through the A to Z of deep learning, it's essential to cast our gaze forward and explore the future of artificial intelligence (AI). The field of AI and deep learning is dynamic, constantly evolving, and poised for remarkable transformations in the coming years. In this section, we'll delve into some of the exciting trends and possibilities that await us on the horizon.

8.3.1. EXPLAINABLE AI (XAI)

One of the pressing challenges in AI is the need for transparency and accountability. Deep learning models, especially complex neural networks, can often be seen as "black boxes" where it's challenging to understand why they make specific decisions. Explainable AI (XAI) is an emerging field that aims to shed light on these black boxes, making AI systems more interpretable and trustworthy.

Here's a simple example of an XAI technique known as Local Interpretable Model-agnostic Explanations (LIME) in Python:

```
from lime.lime_text import
LimeTextExplainer

# Create a LIME explainer for text data

explainer = LimeTextExplainer()

# Explain a prediction made by a deep
learning model

explanation =
explainer.explain_instance(text_to_explain,
deep_learning_model.predict_proba)

# Visualize the explanation

explanation.show_in_notebook()
```

8.3.2. FEDERATED LEARNING

Privacy and data security are paramount concerns in AI, especially when dealing with sensitive information. Federated learning is a decentralized approach that allows machine learning models to be trained across multiple devices or servers while keeping the data localized. This technique enables AI systems to learn from distributed data sources without exposing individual data points.

Here's a high-level overview of federated learning:

```
# Pseudo-code for federated learning

for each device in the network:

    model_copy =
create_copy_of_global_model()

    local_data = get_local_data(device)

    update_local_model(model_copy,
local_data)


    send_local_model_to_global_server(model_cop
y)

    global_model = aggregate_local_models()
```

8.3.3. QUANTUM COMPUTING AND DEEP LEARNING

Quantum computing represents a quantum leap in computing power. While still in its infancy, quantum computers have the potential to revolutionize deep learning by solving complex optimization problems at speeds unattainable by classical computers. Quantum neural networks and quantum machine learning algorithms are actively being researched.

Below is a simplified quantum circuit representation:

```
from qiskit import QuantumCircuit, transpile
```

```
# Create a quantum circuit

circuit = QuantumCircuit(2, 2)

# Apply quantum gates

circuit.h(0)

circuit.cx(0, 1)

circuit.measure([0, 1], [0, 1])

# Compile the circuit for a specific quantum
device

compiled_circuit = transpile(circuit,
backend=device)
```

8.3.4. LIFELONG LEARNING

In the future, AI systems may exhibit more human-like learning capabilities, where they can accumulate knowledge over time and adapt to new tasks without forgetting previously learned information. Lifelong learning, also known as continual learning, is an area of research aiming to achieve this dynamic adaptability.

Here's a conceptual representation of lifelong learning:

```
# Pseudo-code for lifelong learning

while new tasks arrive:

    model.update(new_data)
```

A to Z of Deep Learning

As we conclude this chapter and our journey through the A to Z of deep learning, remember that the future of artificial intelligence is boundless, with countless opportunities for innovation, discovery, and positive impact. Embracing these emerging trends will undoubtedly shape the next generation of intelligent systems.

CHAPTER 9: G FOR GLOSSARY OF DEEP LEARNING TERMS

9.1. DEMYSTIFYING DEEP LEARNING JARGON

Deep learning, like any technical field, comes with its own unique lexicon of terms and acronyms. Understanding this jargon is crucial for grasping the nuances of deep learning and communicating effectively within the community. In this section, we'll unravel some of the most common terms and concepts encountered in the world of deep learning.

1. Artificial Neural Network (ANN):
- Definition: A computational model inspired by the human brain's neural structure, composed of interconnected nodes (neurons) that process information through weighted connections. ANNs are the foundation of deep learning.

2. Backpropagation:
- Definition: An optimization algorithm used to train neural networks by adjusting the weights and biases in reverse order, minimizing the network's error during training.

3. Convolutional Neural Network (CNN):
- Definition: A specialized type of neural network designed for processing grid-like data, such as images and videos. CNNs use convolutional layers to automatically learn hierarchical features from the input data.

4. Deep Learning:

- Definition: A subset of machine learning that involves neural networks with multiple hidden layers. Deep learning models are capable of learning complex patterns and representations from data.

5. Gradient Descent:

- Definition: An iterative optimization algorithm used to find the minimum of a function (typically a loss function) by adjusting model parameters in the direction of the steepest descent.

6. Hyperparameter:

- Definition: A parameter that is not learned from the data but is set prior to training. Examples include learning rates, batch sizes, and the number of layers in a neural network.

7. Overfitting:

- Definition: A phenomenon where a machine learning model performs exceptionally well on the training data but poorly on unseen data. It indicates that the model has learned noise rather than meaningful patterns.

8. ReLU (Rectified Linear Unit):

- Definition: An activation function commonly used in neural networks that replaces negative values with zero and passes positive values unchanged. It helps mitigate the vanishing gradient problem.

9. Supervised Learning:

- Definition: A machine learning paradigm in which the model is trained on labeled data, meaning the input data is paired with corresponding output labels. The goal is to learn a mapping from inputs to outputs.

10. Tensor:

- Definition: A multi-dimensional array used to represent data in deep learning. Tensors can have varying ranks, including scalars (rank-0), vectors (rank-1), matrices (rank-2), and higher-dimensional arrays.

11. Transfer Learning:

- Definition: A technique in which a pre-trained deep learning model is adapted to a new task by fine-tuning some of its layers. This approach leverages knowledge learned from one domain to improve performance in another.

12. Activation Function:

- Definition: A mathematical function applied to the output of a neuron in a neural network. Activation functions introduce non-linearity into the model, allowing it to capture complex patterns in data. Common activation functions include ReLU, Sigmoid, and Tanh.

13. Batch Normalization:

- Definition: A technique used to improve the training stability and convergence of deep neural networks. It normalizes the activations of each layer within a mini-batch, reducing internal covariate shift.

14. Dropout:

- Definition: A regularization technique for neural networks that randomly deactivates a fraction of neurons during training. This helps prevent overfitting by making the network more robust.

15. Loss Function:

- Definition: A mathematical function that measures the difference between the predicted output of a model and the actual target values. The goal during training is to minimize this function.

16. One-Hot Encoding:
- Definition: A technique used to represent categorical data, such as class labels, as binary vectors. Each category is assigned a unique binary code, with one element set to 1 and the others set to 0.

17. RNN (Recurrent Neural Network):
- Definition: A type of neural network architecture designed for sequential data. RNNs have recurrent connections that allow them to maintain internal state and process sequences of variable length.

18. Transfer Function:
- Definition: A function used to calculate the output of a neuron or layer in a neural network. It typically combines the weighted input with an activation function to produce the neuron's output.

19. Unsupervised Learning:
- Definition: A machine learning paradigm where the model learns patterns and structures in data without explicit supervision. Clustering and dimensionality reduction are common tasks in unsupervised learning.

20. Vanishing Gradient Problem:
- Definition: A challenge in training deep neural networks where the gradients of the loss function become very small as they are backpropagated through the layers. This can hinder training progress.

S. Begum

21. Weights and Biases:

- Definition: In the context of neural networks, weights are parameters that determine the strength of connections between neurons, while biases are additional parameters that shift the output of a neuron. They are learned during training.

This glossary serves as a valuable resource for both beginners and experienced practitioners in the field of deep learning. As you dive into the subsequent chapters of this book, you'll encounter these terms and concepts in various contexts, enriching your understanding and equipping you with the knowledge needed to master the A to Z of deep learning.

CHAPTER 10: H FOR HANDS-ON PROJECTS

10.1. PUTTING KNOWLEDGE INTO PRACTICE

In the preceding chapters, you've delved deep into the theory and concepts of deep learning. Now, it's time to roll up your sleeves and put that knowledge to practical use. This hands-on project will guide you through building a simple neural network using Python and a popular deep learning framework, TensorFlow.

Project Objective:
To create a neural network that can classify handwritten digits from the MNIST dataset.

Project Steps:

Step 1: Import the Required Libraries
Before we begin, let's import the necessary libraries. Open your Python environment, and create a new Python script.

```
import tensorflow as tf

from tensorflow import keras

import matplotlib.pyplot as plt
```

Step 2: Load the MNIST Dataset
We'll use the MNIST dataset, a collection of 28x28 pixel grayscale images of handwritten digits (0-9).

```
mnist = keras.datasets.mnist

(train_images, train_labels), (test_images,
test_labels) = mnist.load_data()
```

Step 3: Preprocess the Data

Neural networks work best with normalized data. We'll scale the pixel values from 0-255 to a range of 0-1.

```
train_images, test_images = train_images /
255.0, test_images / 255.0
```

Step 4: Build the Neural Network

Let's create a simple feedforward neural network with one hidden layer.

```
model = keras.Sequential([

    keras.layers.Flatten(input_shape=(28, 28)),

    keras.layers.Dense(128, activation='relu'),

    keras.layers.Dropout(0.2),

    keras.layers.Dense(10,
activation='softmax')

])
```

Step 5: Compile the Model

Compile the model, specifying the optimizer, loss function, and metrics to track during training.

```
model.compile(optimizer='adam',

        loss='sparse_categorical_crossentropy',

        metrics=['accuracy'])
```

Step 6: Train the Model
Now, train the model on the training data.

```
model.fit(train_images, train_labels,
epochs=5)
```

Step 7: Evaluate the Model
Evaluate the model's performance on the test data.

```
test_loss, test_acc =
model.evaluate(test_images, test_labels,
verbose=2)

print(f"\nTest accuracy:
{test_acc*100:.2f}%")
```

Step 8: Make Predictions
Finally, let's make predictions using our trained model.

```
predictions = model.predict(test_images)
```

Congratulations! You've completed a practical deep learning project. You've built a neural network that can recognize handwritten digits. This is just the beginning of your journey into the fascinating world of deep learning. Feel free to explore more complex projects and continue your exploration of the A to Z of deep learning.

In the following sections of this chapter, we'll dive into more hands-on projects and explore real-world applications of deep learning. Stay curious and keep experimenting!

10.2. BUILDING YOUR FIRST NEURAL NETWORK

In this chapter, we embark on a practical journey to help you build your very first neural network from scratch. We'll guide you through the fundamental steps, providing both theoretical insights and hands-on code examples. By the end of this section, you'll have a solid understanding of the key components that make up a neural network and be well-prepared to create your own deep learning models.

UNDERSTANDING NEURAL NETWORKS

Before diving into the code, let's grasp the core concept of a neural network. At its heart, a neural network is a computational model inspired by the human brain. It consists of interconnected layers of artificial neurons, also known as nodes or units. These neurons work together to process and transform data, enabling the network to make predictions, classify objects, or solve complex problems.

SETTING UP THE ENVIRONMENT

To begin, you need the appropriate tools and libraries. We recommend using Python and a deep learning framework

A to Z of Deep Learning

such as TensorFlow or PyTorch. Ensure you have these libraries installed, as well as any dependencies for your specific project.

Here's a simple Python script to import TensorFlow:

```
import tensorflow as tf
```

CREATING THE NEURAL NETWORK

Now, let's construct a basic neural network. For simplicity, we'll build a feedforward neural network, also known as a multi-layer perceptron. This network consists of an input layer, one or more hidden layers, and an output layer.

Here's a code snippet to create a simple neural network using TensorFlow's Keras API:

```
# Import necessary modules

import tensorflow as tf

from tensorflow import keras

from tensorflow.keras import layers


# Define the model

model = keras.Sequential([
```

```
    layers.Input(shape=(input_dim,)),    # Input
layer

    layers.Dense(128, activation='relu'), #
Hidden layer with 128 neurons and ReLU
activation

    layers.Dense(64, activation='relu'),  #
Another hidden layer with 64 neurons and
ReLU activation

    layers.Dense(output_dim,
activation='softmax')  # Output layer

])

# Compile the model

model.compile(optimizer='adam',
loss='categorical_crossentropy',
metrics=['accuracy'])
```

In this code, we've created a simple feedforward neural network with two hidden layers. The `input_dim` and `output_dim` should be replaced with the appropriate dimensions for your specific task.

TRAINING THE NEURAL NETWORK

Once you've defined your neural network, the next step is to train it using data. You'll need labeled data for supervised learning tasks. Here's a simplified example of training your model:

```
# Load your training data (X_train, y_train)


# Train the model

model.fit(X_train, y_train, epochs=10,
batch_size=32)
```

In this snippet, `X_train` represents your training data features, and `y_train` represents the corresponding labels. Adjust the number of epochs and batch size according to your problem.

EVALUATING YOUR MODEL

After training, it's crucial to evaluate your model's performance using a separate test dataset:

```
# Load your test data (X_test, y_test)

# Evaluate the model

test_loss, test_accuracy =
model.evaluate(X_test, y_test)

print(f"Test Loss: {test_loss:.4f}")

print(f"Test Accuracy:
{test_accuracy*100:.2f}%")
```

This code will provide you with insights into how well your neural network generalizes to unseen data.

Building your first neural network is an exciting step in your deep learning journey. In this section, we've introduced you to the fundamental concepts and provided a hands-on example using TensorFlow and Keras. Feel free to experiment with different architectures, datasets, and hyperparameters as you continue to explore the world of deep learning.

10.3. REAL-WORLD APPLICATIONS OF DEEP LEARNING

In the previous sections of this book, we've delved deep into the theory and concepts that underlie deep learning. Now, it's time to bring that knowledge to life through real-world applications. In this section, we'll explore some tangible projects that showcase the incredible potential of deep learning across various domains.

10.3.1. IMAGE CLASSIFICATION WITH CONVOLUTIONAL NEURAL NETWORKS (CNNS)

Let's start with a classic deep learning task: image classification using Convolutional Neural Networks (CNNs). This project will teach you how to train a model to recognize objects in images. We'll use popular deep learning frameworks like TensorFlow or PyTorch to build and train our CNN. Here's a simplified Python code snippet to get you started:

```
import tensorflow as tf

from tensorflow.keras import layers, models
```

```python
# Load your dataset (e.g., CIFAR-10)

(train_images, train_labels), (test_images,
test_labels) =
tf.keras.datasets.cifar10.load_data()


# Preprocess the data

train_images, test_images = train_images /
255.0, test_images / 255.0


# Build a simple CNN model

model = models.Sequential([

    layers.Conv2D(32, (3, 3), activation='relu',
input_shape=(32, 32, 3)),

    layers.MaxPooling2D((2, 2)),

    layers.Conv2D(64, (3, 3), activation='relu'),

    layers.MaxPooling2D((2, 2)),

    layers.Conv2D(64, (3, 3), activation='relu'),

    layers.Flatten(),

    layers.Dense(64, activation='relu'),

    layers.Dense(10)

])
```

```python
# Compile the model

model.compile(optimizer='adam',

loss=tf.keras.losses.SparseCategoricalCrossent
ropy(from_logits=True),

                metrics=['accuracy'])


# Train the model

model.fit(train_images, train_labels,
epochs=10, validation_data=(test_images,
test_labels))
```

This hands-on project will provide you with a practical understanding of how deep learning can be applied to image recognition tasks.

10.3.2. NATURAL LANGUAGE PROCESSING (NLP) FOR SENTIMENT ANALYSIS

Moving beyond images, let's explore natural language processing (NLP) with a sentiment analysis project. In this project, you'll learn how to use deep learning techniques to analyze text data and determine sentiment (positive, negative, or neutral). Here's a glimpse of how you can build a simple sentiment analysis model using Python and libraries like TensorFlow or PyTorch:

A to Z of Deep Learning

```python
import tensorflow as tf

from tensorflow.keras.preprocessing.text import Tokenizer

from tensorflow.keras.preprocessing.sequence import pad_sequences

# Load your dataset (e.g., movie reviews)

(train_texts, train_labels), (test_texts, test_labels) = load_and_preprocess_data()

# Tokenize and pad the text data

tokenizer = Tokenizer(num_words=10000, oov_token="<OOV>")

tokenizer.fit_on_texts(train_texts)

word_index = tokenizer.word_index

train_sequences = tokenizer.texts_to_sequences(train_texts)

train_padded = pad_sequences(train_sequences, maxlen=100, padding='post', truncating='post')

# Build an NLP model (e.g., using LSTM or Transformer)

model = build_nlp_model()

# Compile the model

model.compile(loss='binary_crossentropy',
```

```
        optimizer='adam',

        metrics=['accuracy'])

    # Train the model

    model.fit(train_padded, train_labels,
    epochs=5, validation_split=0.2)
```

This project will give you a hands-on experience of applying deep learning to text data and understanding sentiment analysis.

10.3.3. AUTONOMOUS ROBOT NAVIGATION

Lastly, let's dive into a more complex application: autonomous robot navigation. In this project, you'll learn how deep reinforcement learning can be used to train a robot to navigate and make decisions in a dynamic environment. While the code for this project can be extensive and hardware-dependent, it's a fascinating journey into the intersection of deep learning and robotics.

These real-world projects are just the tip of the iceberg when it comes to the practical applications of deep learning. By working through these examples, you'll gain valuable insights and skills that can be applied to a wide range of exciting and impactful projects.

In the following chapters, we'll wrap up our journey through the A to Z of deep learning, reflecting on what you've learned and exploring the future of this dynamic field.

CHAPTER 11: I FOR INDUSTRY APPLICATIONS

11.1. DEEP LEARNING IN HEALTHCARE

In the realm of deep learning, few sectors hold as much promise and potential as healthcare. The marriage of advanced neural networks and the vast amount of medical data available is revolutionizing the way we diagnose, treat, and manage diseases. This chapter explores the profound impact of deep learning in healthcare and unveils some of the most remarkable applications reshaping the medical landscape.

UNDERSTANDING THE HEALTHCARE CHALLENGE

The healthcare industry faces significant challenges, including the need for faster and more accurate diagnoses, personalized treatment plans, and the effective management of patient records. Deep learning, with its ability to analyze complex patterns in data, has emerged as a powerful ally in overcoming these challenges.

MEDICAL IMAGING WITH CONVOLUTIONAL NEURAL NETWORKS (CNNS)

One of the standout applications of deep learning in healthcare is the use of Convolutional Neural Networks (CNNs) for medical image analysis. These networks excel at tasks such as:

S. Begum

- X-ray and CT Scan Interpretation: CNNs can identify abnormalities in X-rays and CT scans, aiding radiologists in detecting conditions like lung cancer, fractures, or tumors.

```
# Example CNN code for X-ray classification

import tensorflow as tf

model = tf.keras.Sequential([

    tf.keras.layers.Conv2D(64, (3, 3), activation='relu', input_shape=(256, 256, 3)),

    tf.keras.layers.MaxPooling2D(2, 2),

    tf.keras.layers.Flatten(),

    tf.keras.layers.Dense(2, activation='softmax')

])
```

- MRI Image Segmentation: CNNs can segment MRI images to isolate specific structures or regions of interest, crucial for planning surgeries or assessing the progression of diseases like multiple sclerosis.

```
# Example CNN code for MRI image segmentation

import tensorflow as tf
```

A to Z of Deep Learning

```
model = tf.keras.Sequential([

    tf.keras.layers.Conv2D(64, (3, 3),
    activation='relu', input_shape=(256, 256, 1)),

    tf.keras.layers.MaxPooling2D(2, 2),

    tf.keras.layers.Conv2D(128, (3, 3),
    activation='relu'),

    tf.keras.layers.MaxPooling2D(2, 2),

    tf.keras.layers.Flatten(),

    tf.keras.layers.Dense(2,
    activation='softmax')

])
```

- Pathological Image Analysis: Deep learning is also being used to analyze histopathological images, assisting pathologists in diagnosing diseases like cancer with higher accuracy.

DRUG DISCOVERY AND GENOMICS

Deep learning plays a crucial role in accelerating drug discovery and genomics research. It can analyze vast genomic datasets to identify potential drug candidates, predict how a drug will interact with specific proteins, and even aid in designing personalized treatment plans based on an individual's genetic makeup.

S. Begum

ELECTRONIC HEALTH RECORDS (EHR) MANAGEMENT

Managing electronic health records (EHR) is a complex task in healthcare. Deep learning algorithms can help automate the extraction of valuable insights from EHRs, enabling healthcare providers to make more informed decisions and improve patient care.

CHALLENGES AND ETHICAL CONSIDERATIONS

While the benefits of deep learning in healthcare are immense, they come with challenges such as data privacy, regulatory compliance, and ethical concerns. It's vital to strike a balance between innovation and patient well-being, ensuring that AI systems are transparent, secure, and unbiased.

In this chapter, we'll delve deeper into each of these applications, providing real-world examples, code snippets, and insights into the future of deep learning in healthcare. By the end, you'll have a comprehensive understanding of how deep learning is transforming the healthcare industry and improving the quality of care for patients worldwide.

NATURAL LANGUAGE PROCESSING (NLP) FOR MEDICAL TEXTS

Beyond medical imaging and genomics, deep learning techniques have found a valuable niche in the analysis of medical texts. Natural Language Processing (NLP) models can extract meaningful information from unstructured medical records, research papers, and clinical notes.

A to Z of Deep Learning

- Clinical Decision Support: NLP-powered models can assist clinicians in making decisions by parsing patient records and highlighting relevant information, potential diagnoses, and treatment options.

```python
# Example NLP code for clinical text analysis

import transformers

tokenizer = transformers.AutoTokenizer.from_pretrained("bert-base-uncased")

model = transformers.AutoModelForSequenceClassification.from_pretrained("bert-base-uncased")

input_text = "Patient presents with chest pain and shortness of breath. No known allergies."

input_ids = tokenizer.encode(input_text, add_special_tokens=True, truncation=True, padding=True, return_tensors="pt")

output = model(input_ids)
```

- Drug Information Extraction: NLP models can extract drug-related information from medical literature, aiding pharmacovigilance and drug development.

- Medical Literature Summarization: Deep learning models can summarize extensive medical research papers, making it easier for healthcare professionals to stay updated with the latest findings.

S. Begum

REMOTE MONITORING AND PREDICTIVE ANALYTICS

In the era of telehealth and remote patient monitoring, deep learning contributes significantly. Wearable devices and sensors collect a wealth of health-related data, which can be analyzed to predict health events, monitor chronic conditions, and provide timely interventions.

- Early Disease Detection: Deep learning algorithms can analyze continuous streams of patient data to detect early signs of conditions like diabetes or heart disease, enabling proactive healthcare.

```
# Example code for time series analysis in
remote monitoring

import tensorflow as tf

model = tf.keras.Sequential([

    tf.keras.layers.LSTM(64, input_shape=(30,
1)),

    tf.keras.layers.Dense(1,
activation='sigmoid')

])
```

THE HUMAN-AI PARTNERSHIP

It's essential to emphasize that deep learning doesn't replace healthcare professionals but enhances their capabilities. The synergy between human expertise and AI-driven insights is at the heart of these applications. In the following sections of this chapter, we will explore case studies, practical implementations, and ethical considerations surrounding deep learning in healthcare.

The integration of deep learning into healthcare represents a profound transformation. It empowers healthcare providers to make more accurate diagnoses, discover new treatments, and manage patient data more effectively. However, this transformation comes with challenges and responsibilities, from ensuring data security to addressing ethical concerns. In this chapter, we will navigate the intricacies of deep learning's role in healthcare, providing you with a comprehensive understanding of its potential and limitations.

11.2. TRANSFORMING FINANCE WITH DEEP LEARNING

In the realm of finance, where precision and insight can be the difference between success and failure, deep learning has emerged as a transformative force. In this chapter, we will delve into how deep learning techniques are reshaping the financial industry, from trading algorithms to risk assessment and fraud detection.

UNDERSTANDING THE LANDSCAPE

The financial sector thrives on data, and deep learning excels in extracting valuable insights from vast datasets. Here, we will explore some key applications:

1. Algorithmic Trading: Deep learning models are being deployed to analyze market trends, news sentiment, and historical data to make split-second trading decisions. These models can recognize complex patterns that human traders might miss.

2. Risk Assessment: Assessing the risk associated with loans, investments, or insurance policies is a critical task. Deep learning models can analyze a borrower's credit history, economic indicators, and even social media data to gauge their creditworthiness more accurately.

3. Fraud Detection: Financial institutions are using deep learning to detect fraudulent activities. By analyzing transaction patterns, user behaviors, and anomaly detection, these models can flag potentially fraudulent transactions in real time.

4. Portfolio Management: Deep learning models can assist in optimizing investment portfolios. They can consider various factors, such as risk tolerance and market conditions, to recommend the most suitable investment strategies.

PRACTICAL IMPLEMENTATION

Let's take a look at a simplified example of using a recurrent neural network (RNN) for time-series forecasting in finance. In this case, we'll predict stock prices, a classic use case.

```
import numpy as np

import pandas as pd
```

```python
import tensorflow as tf

from sklearn.preprocessing import
MinMaxScaler

from tensorflow.keras.models import
Sequential

from tensorflow.keras.layers import LSTM,
Dense

# Load historical stock data

data = pd.read_csv('stock_prices.csv')

prices = data['Close'].values.reshape(-1, 1)

# Normalize data

scaler = MinMaxScaler()

prices_scaled = scaler.fit_transform(prices)

# Create sequences for training

sequence_length = 30

X, y = [], []

for i in range(len(prices_scaled) -
sequence_length):

    X.append(prices_scaled[i:i+sequence_length])

    y.append(prices_scaled[i+sequence_length])
```

```
X = np.array(X)

y = np.array(y)

# Split data into training and testing sets

train_size = int(len(X) * 0.8)

X_train, X_test, y_train, y_test =
X[:train_size], X[train_size:], y[:train_size],
y[train_size:]

# Build an LSTM model

model = Sequential()

model.add(LSTM(50, activation='relu',
input_shape=(sequence_length, 1)))

model.add(Dense(1))

model.compile(optimizer='adam',
loss='mean_squared_error')

# Train the model

model.fit(X_train, y_train, epochs=10,
batch_size=32)

# Evaluate the model

loss = model.evaluate(X_test, y_test)

print(f"Mean Squared Error: {loss}")
```

This example demonstrates the application of deep learning in predicting stock prices by training an LSTM neural network on historical data.

The marriage of deep learning and finance is poised to revolutionize the industry. Whether it's making trading decisions, assessing risk, detecting fraud, or optimizing portfolios, deep learning's ability to extract insights from data is proving invaluable. As you continue your journey through the A to Z of deep learning, keep in mind that its applications are boundless, and the financial sector is just one of many beneficiaries.

11.3. DEEP LEARNING IN AUTONOMOUS VEHICLES

In recent years, the world has witnessed an automotive revolution driven by the integration of deep learning into autonomous vehicles. This section explores the fascinating role that deep learning plays in the development and operation of self-driving cars. As we delve into the world of autonomous vehicles, you'll discover how deep learning algorithms are transforming the way we commute and envision the future of transportation.

UNDERSTANDING THE AUTONOMOUS VEHICLE ECOSYSTEM

Before we dive into the deep learning aspects, it's crucial to grasp the broader landscape of autonomous vehicles. Autonomous vehicles, often referred to as self-driving cars or driverless cars, are vehicles capable of navigating and operating without human intervention. They rely on a complex ecosystem of hardware and software components, including sensors (such as LiDAR and cameras), control systems, and, of course, deep learning algorithms.

SENSORS AND DATA COLLECTION

Autonomous vehicles are equipped with an array of sensors that continually collect data from the vehicle's surroundings. LiDAR (Light Detection and Ranging) sensors use lasers to measure distances to objects, creating detailed 3D maps of the environment. Cameras capture images and videos, while radar sensors detect the speed and location of nearby objects.

```
# Sample code for LiDAR data collection

import lidar

lidar_sensor = lidar.LiDAR()

lidar_data = lidar_sensor.get_data()
```

DEEP LEARNING FOR PERCEPTION

Deep learning plays a pivotal role in enabling autonomous vehicles to perceive and interpret the world around them. Convolutional Neural Networks (CNNs) are commonly used to process the data from cameras and LiDAR sensors. These networks can identify pedestrians, other vehicles, road signs, and even lane markings.

```
# Sample code for object detection using a CNN
```

A to Z of Deep Learning

```
import tensorflow as tf

from tensorflow.keras.applications import
MobileNetV2

# Load a pre-trained CNN model

model = MobileNetV2(weights='imagenet')

# Process an image from the camera

image = load_image_from_camera()

predictions = model.predict(image)
```

PATH PLANNING AND CONTROL

Once perception is established, deep learning algorithms assist in path planning and control. Reinforcement learning techniques can be used to teach the vehicle how to navigate safely, obey traffic rules, and make complex decisions.

```
# Sample code for reinforcement learning

import gym

import tensorflow as tf

from tensorflow.keras import layers

# Define a reinforcement learning
environment

env = gym.make('AutonomousCar-v1')
```

```
# Create a deep Q-network (DQN)

model = tf.keras.Sequential([

    layers.Dense(24, activation='relu'),

    layers.Dense(24, activation='relu'),

    layers.Dense(env.action_space.n)

])
```

CHALLENGES AND FUTURE PROSPECTS

While deep learning has brought us closer to the realization of autonomous vehicles, numerous challenges remain. These include handling adverse weather conditions, ensuring cybersecurity, and addressing the ethical implications of autonomous vehicles' decision-making.

The future of autonomous vehicles holds great promise. As deep learning algorithms continue to evolve and improve, we can anticipate safer, more efficient transportation systems, reduced accidents, and increased accessibility for people with mobility challenges. The journey towards fully autonomous vehicles powered by deep learning is an exciting one, with boundless possibilities on the horizon.

In the next chapter, we'll conclude our exploration of the A to Z of deep learning, reflecting on the incredible journey we've embarked upon and considering the endless opportunities that await in this ever-evolving field.

CHAPTER 12: J FOR JOURNEY'S END AND BEYOND

12.1. RECAP AND REFLECTION

As we draw near to the conclusion of our journey through the A to Z of deep learning, it's essential to take a moment to reflect on the incredible terrain we've covered. This chapter serves as a virtual pit stop, allowing you to pause and recapitulate the key insights and concepts you've encountered on this intellectual expedition.

12.1.1. THE DEEP LEARNING LANDSCAPE

Throughout this book, we've delved into the intricate landscape of deep learning. From its inception to its far-reaching applications, we've explored the fundamental building blocks, the mathematical underpinnings, and the tools and frameworks that make it all possible. You've gained a firm understanding of neural networks, activation functions, backpropagation, and convolutional neural networks (CNNs), among other critical topics.

12.1.2. PRACTICAL IMPLEMENTATION

But knowledge alone is not enough. We've also ventured into the practical realm, where you've learned how to set up your deep learning environment, harness the power of Python libraries, and work with real-world data. Remember your first neural network? You've come a long way since then, and you're now equipped to tackle complex projects and challenges in the field.

```
# Example: Building a simple neural network in Python

import tensorflow as tf

from tensorflow import keras

model = keras.Sequential([

    keras.layers.Dense(128, activation='relu', input_shape=(784,)),

    keras.layers.Dropout(0.2),

    keras.layers.Dense(10, activation='softmax')

])

model.compile(optimizer='adam',

        loss='sparse_categorical_crossentropy',

        metrics=['accuracy'])
```

12.1.3. ETHICAL CONSIDERATIONS

We've also touched upon the ethical dimensions of deep learning. In an age where AI technologies are reshaping society, it's crucial to be aware of issues related to bias, fairness, privacy, and security. As a responsible practitioner, you now have the knowledge to navigate these challenging waters with a keen ethical compass.

12.1.4. THE FUTURE BECKONS

As we reflect on the journey thus far, remember that your exploration of deep learning doesn't end here. The field is dynamic and ever-evolving. Emerging trends, such as quantum computing and novel architectures, promise exciting opportunities for innovation and discovery.

In the chapters ahead, we'll discuss the future of deep learning, including its implications for various industries and its potential to reshape the world as we know it. The journey may be coming to a close, but the path forward is filled with endless possibilities.

Take a moment to ponder your own journey through the A to Z of deep learning. What discoveries have fascinated you the most? What challenges have you overcome? As we embark on the final leg of our expedition, keep these reflections in mind, for they will serve as a compass guiding you into the uncharted territories of the future.

In the next section, we'll explore how you can continue your deep learning odyssey, armed with the knowledge and skills you've acquired on this remarkable journey. The adventure is far from over, and the possibilities are limitless.

12.2: CONTINUING YOUR DEEP LEARNING ODYSSEY

Congratulations on embarking on this journey through the A to Z of deep learning! By now, you've gained valuable insights into the world of artificial intelligence, neural networks, and the remarkable applications of deep learning. As we wrap up this adventure, it's important to consider how you can continue your exploration and stay current in this rapidly evolving field.

12.2.1. STAY INFORMED

Deep learning is a field that's constantly evolving. New research papers, techniques, and tools are released regularly. To stay informed, consider the following:

- Research Papers: Keep an eye on reputable journals and conferences in the field of deep learning, such as NeurIPS, ICML, and CVPR. Reading research papers will help you understand the latest developments.

- Blogs and Newsletters: Many experts and organizations maintain blogs and newsletters that provide insights into recent developments. Subscribe to these sources to receive regular updates.

12.2.2. COLLABORATE AND JOIN COMMUNITIES

Deep learning is often a collaborative endeavor. Engage with the community to share your knowledge, seek advice, and collaborate on projects. Here's how:

- Online Forums: Websites like Stack Overflow and Reddit's r/MachineLearning are great places to ask questions and share your expertise.

A to Z of Deep Learning

- Meetups and Conferences: Attend local meetups and conferences related to AI and deep learning. These events provide networking opportunities and a chance to learn from experts.

12.2.3. EXPLORE ADVANCED TOPICS

Deep learning offers a vast landscape of advanced topics to explore. Consider delving deeper into areas such as:

- Reinforcement Learning: Learn how to train agents to make decisions in dynamic environments.

- Natural Language Processing (NLP): Dive into the world of text and language understanding using deep learning.

12.2.4. CONTRIBUTE TO OPEN SOURCE

Consider contributing to open-source deep learning projects. By collaborating with the community, you can both learn and give back to the field. Platforms like GitHub host numerous open-source projects related to deep learning.

In conclusion, your deep learning journey is far from over; it's a lifelong odyssey filled with exciting discoveries and challenges. By staying informed, engaging with the community, exploring advanced topics, and contributing to open source, you can continue to unlock the depths of intelligence and make your mark in the world of deep learning. Remember, the possibilities are boundless, and the future of AI is in your hands. Happy learning!

12.3. THE EVER-EVOLVING WORLD OF DEEP LEARNING

As you've embarked on this journey through the A to Z of deep learning, you've gained valuable insights into the foundations, techniques, and applications of this dynamic field. However, it's important to recognize that deep learning is a constantly evolving domain. What you've learned so far is just the tip of the iceberg in this ever-expanding universe of artificial intelligence.

Deep learning has a bright and exciting future ahead, and in this concluding chapter, we'll explore some of the current trends and future directions that are shaping the field.

CURRENT TRENDS IN DEEP LEARNING

Transfer Learning: One of the remarkable trends in deep learning is transfer learning. Models pre-trained on massive datasets are fine-tuned for specific tasks, enabling faster and more efficient learning for various applications. This approach has been a game-changer in natural language processing, computer vision, and more.

Explainable AI: As deep learning systems become more complex, the need for interpretability and transparency is growing. Researchers are working on techniques to make deep learning models more understandable, allowing us to trust and explain their decisions.

A to Z of Deep Learning

AI for Healthcare: Deep learning is revolutionizing healthcare by assisting in disease diagnosis, drug discovery, and personalized medicine. Expect to see more breakthroughs in this field, potentially saving countless lives.

Autonomous Systems: From self-driving cars to drones, deep learning is at the heart of autonomous systems. The ongoing development of robust, safe, and efficient AI-powered vehicles will continue to be a focus.

FUTURE DIRECTIONS IN DEEP LEARNING

Quantum Computing: Quantum computing holds the promise of tackling complex deep learning tasks at speeds that were once unimaginable. As quantum technologies mature, they will likely play a pivotal role in advancing the field.

Neuromorphic Computing: Inspired by the human brain, neuromorphic computing aims to build hardware that mimics the brain's architecture. This could lead to highly efficient and adaptive deep learning systems.

Ethics and Regulations: As AI becomes more integrated into society, ethical considerations and regulations will play a pivotal role. Expect discussions and developments in AI ethics and governance to intensify.

Human-AI Collaboration: Deep learning systems will increasingly work alongside humans, enhancing our abilities in decision-making, creativity, and problem-solving. Human-AI symbiosis will be a focus of research and development.

S. Begum

CONTINUING YOUR DEEP LEARNING ODYSSEY

The journey you've embarked upon is far from over. To stay at the forefront of deep learning, consider the following steps:

1. Stay Informed: Continuously update your knowledge by following research papers, attending conferences, and joining online communities.

2. Experiment and Innovate: Don't be afraid to experiment with new ideas and technologies. Innovation often comes from trying the unconventional.

3. Collaborate: Deep learning is a collaborative field. Engage with others, share your insights, and learn from their experiences.

4. Teach and Mentor: Sharing your knowledge with others not only reinforces your understanding but also contributes to the growth of the deep learning community.

As we conclude this journey, remember that deep learning is a field where curiosity knows no bounds. The depths of intelligence you can unlock are limited only by your imagination and dedication. Embrace the ever-evolving world of deep learning and continue to push the boundaries of what's possible.

In the words of Alan Turing, "We can only see a short distance ahead, but we can see plenty there that needs to be done." The future of deep learning is in your hands.

CONCLUSION: CELEBRATING YOUR JOURNEY THROUGH DEEP LEARNING

As we draw our exploration of the A to Z of deep learning to a close, it's time to reflect on the incredible journey you've undertaken. You've ventured into the world of artificial intelligence and neural networks, delving into the complexities and possibilities of deep learning. Along the way, you've unlocked the depths of intelligence and gained insights into the inner workings of this transformative field.

In this concluding chapter, we want to celebrate your achievements and provide some key takeaways to carry with you as you continue your deep learning odyssey.

1. MASTERY OF FUNDAMENTALS

You've acquired a solid foundation in deep learning, understanding the core concepts, terminologies, and mathematical underpinnings. You now know what neural networks are, how they learn, and why deep learning is a game-changer in the world of artificial intelligence.

2. HANDS-ON EXPERIENCE

Throughout this journey, you've not just been a passive observer but an active participant. You've likely implemented neural networks, trained models, and solved real-world problems. Your hands-on experience is invaluable.

3. ETHICAL CONSIDERATIONS

You've also gained an understanding of the ethical challenges that deep learning presents. You're equipped to navigate the complexities of bias, fairness, and privacy, ensuring that your deep learning endeavors align with ethical standards.

4. REAL-WORLD APPLICATIONS

Deep learning is not just an abstract concept; it has tangible applications in various industries. You've explored how it's being used in healthcare, finance, autonomous vehicles, and more. Your knowledge can drive innovation in these fields.

5. CONTINUOUS LEARNING

The field of deep learning is dynamic and ever-evolving. As you celebrate your achievements, remember that your journey doesn't end here. Continue to stay updated with the latest research, technologies, and trends in the deep learning landscape.

6. COLLABORATIVE SPIRIT

Deep learning thrives in a collaborative environment. Whether you're a researcher, developer, or enthusiast, collaboration with peers, mentors, and experts can amplify your impact.

A to Z of Deep Learning

In closing, "A Journey Through the A to Z of Deep Learning: Unlocking the Depths of Intelligence" has been a guide to empower you in the world of deep learning. It's a testament to your dedication and curiosity. Your journey doesn't end here; it's a stepping stone to new discoveries, innovations, and contributions to the exciting field of deep learning.

As you embark on the next phase of your deep learning adventure, remember that the quest for knowledge is boundless, and the depths of intelligence are waiting to be unlocked by individuals like you. Keep exploring, keep learning, and keep pushing the boundaries of what's possible with deep learning. The future is yours to shape.